MW00883077

ISBN: 9781720129684

Printed in the United States of America

10 9 8 7 6 5 4 3 2 1

Construction Project Essentials

Table of Contents

Overview of the 5 Step 4PM Methodology

I've titled this book <u>Construction Project Essentials</u> and it's just that. We're going to take you through a five-step process for

Construction Project Essentials

planning projects, developing a work breakdown structure, building a dynamic schedule, assigning crews/subs to tasks and tracking results. You will learn these techniques on a project for a remodel of an office space with other achievements that must take place in the remodeled space.

 There are things this book will not teach you. We won't deal with the statistics of risk or the alternative ways to develop work estimates or the cost accounting required for project budgets. You'll learn the essence of project management but not all of the detailed information in the Project Management Body of Knowledge (PMBOK®). I wrote this book for people running smaller projects with most of the project crews coming from their own organization.

You'll also learn to use project management software in a very straightforward, simple way. This book has many illustrations of applying this simple methodology in Microsoft Project®. Using project management software with this simple methodology is a big time saver so we recommend that approach. Our objective is not to spend a lot of time in the software. I designed the methodology so you spend only an hour or two developing the plan & schedule and then 10 or 15 minutes a week using the software to update it. You'll spend the rest of your time managing the project.

In sum, Construction Project Essentials teaches you basic-level project management tools and techniques. It's appropriate for smaller construction projects with a three to five crews/subs. Our more advanced publications like Managing Information Technology Projects, Managing Healthcare Projects, Managing Construction Projects and Advanced Project Management

Construction Project Essentials

<u>Techniques</u> address the techniques required for managing larger, more complex projects.

5-Step 4PM Process

We've listed the 5 steps in the process on the chart on the next page along with the 12 best practices techniques you will learn. We're going to take you through a five-step process for planning projects, developing a work breakdown structure, building a dynamic schedule, assigning crews/subs to tasks and tracking results.

As you move through those five steps, you'll learn 12 best practice techniques for delivering projects on time. You'll go through the process of working with the Customer and other interested parties who will be affected by your project (we'll call them project stakeholders).

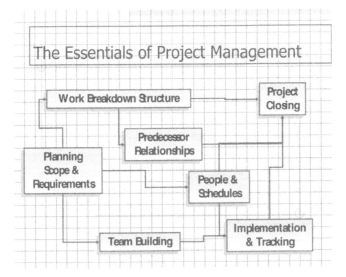

Construction Project Essentials

12 Best Practice Techniques You'll Learn:

1. Defining the Project Scope As a Measured Business Result
2. Decomposing the Scope into a Deliverable Network
3. Avoiding Problems with the Project Charter
4. Using Project Software in 10 Minutes a Week
5. Decomposing Deliverables into a Work Breakdown Structure
6. Sequencing Your Tasks to Finish As Early As Possible
7. Making Clear Assignments to Your Project Crews
8. Using the Critical Path to Optimize Your Schedule
9. Leading a High-Performance Crews
10. Using the Baseline to Spot Problems Early
11. Solving Problems and Reporting to the Customer
12. Closing Projects to Make the Next One Easier

Construction Project Essentials

Key Outputs from the 5-step Process

Broadbrush Project Plan

The Broadbrush Plan is a concise 1½-page document for project initiation. It allows Customers to make decisions and exercise strategic control over projects and the business value they produce. It also provides them with hard-edged metrics for measuring performance and the quality of the deliverables.

Scope & High-Level Deliverable Network

This network of deliverables is the path from where you are now to where you want to be, which is the scope of the project. Every entry in the network is a deliverable that you define with a metric. The metric tells everyone what you will produce and how you will define success.

Work Breakdown Structure Decomposition

Rather than creating mindless "to do" lists, project managers (PMs) craft work breakdown structures by breaking down the scope into a high-level deliverable network of measurable results that become crews/subs' accountabilities. Every crew or sub's assignment is in the form of a measurable business outcome so their accountability is crystal clear. The resulting WBS is compact so the PM can control the scope and update it quickly and control the project scope. You will support each entry with a work package that makes the details clear so they miss nothing. The PM and the Customer have unambiguous checkpoints to measure progress.

Dynamic Project Scheduling

PMs use dynamic project scheduling techniques that let them update plans in just minutes each week and quickly model alternatives to cut duration, lower budgets and adjust the business value a project produces. These techniques give Customers the hard data they need for decision-making and consideration of alternatives.

Status Reporting with Clear Checkpoints

With weekly tracking, PMs and Customers have hard-edged checkpoints to measure progress. They can anticipate problems and implement corrective action early, when it costs the least. PMs make concise status reports on projects and always offer alternatives for the Customer to consider.

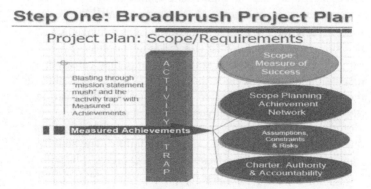

Step One: Broadbrush Project Plan

Step One: Broadbrush Plan

You will start your project management work by defining the scope of the project with the Customer. That is, you'll define the business objective the Customer wants the project to deliver. When you set about defining the scope during project planning there are a number of traps to avoid. One trap is thinking about what you have to do rather than the project's end results. Thinking about the activities you need to complete is much easier than thinking about the business outcome the project should produce. This is the activity trap where you focus on the details and ignore the project's business purpose. In the activity trap, a PM receives a project assignment, thinks about the first thing to do and starts work, figuring to think about the next step when they come to it.

Sometimes, PMs cloak their descent into the activity trap by writing a long and flowery mission statement for the project. This does no harm unless it is a substitute for politely pushing the Customer to make the hard "end result" decisions up front. You need to specify exactly what the project **will** deliver and what it **will not** deliver. The Customer has to make this decision and tell you how he will judge the success of the project. Being that explicit at the beginning may cause some discussion and disagreement but it is far better to work through those conflicts before you start work rather than discovering the success measures when you are almost done. Unfortunately, the activity trap snares so many PMs that it is one of the two leading causes of project failure. The activity trap wastes resources and frustrates project crews/subs with continuously changing assignments. The lure of the activity trap, that bottomless pit, has ruined countless projects.

Top-Down Project Planning

You'll avoid the activity trap with a 1-2 page document, called the Broadbrush plan, which covers the big-picture decisions that are required before you can start your project. When the project Customer and stakeholders approve the Broadbrush plan, the Initiation phase of the project is complete. The key to this process is to avoid those delicious technical details that quickly drag you into the "activity trap." Your focus during a Broadbrush planning process is to provide the Customer with the opportunity to make decisions about the end results the project will produce. Your focus is on the measured business-relevant outcomes not the details of how you will achieve them. You also want to secure the Customer's decisions on the authority you'll need to manage the project crews and subs. You keep the document short and high-level so you engage their attention. You can develop long formal plans later when the Customer has approved the strategy.

A Broadbrush project plan is never long but requires thought, decisions and agreement on three things:

1. Project Scope - an unambiguous measurement of the project's outcome. For example, "Answer 90% of our customers' inquiries in 120 seconds or less with no more than 5% callbacks on the same problem."

2. High-level Deliverable Network (HLD) - a hierarchical network of measured deliverables that leads to the scope.

3. Project Charter – a short narrative covering risks, assumptions, constraints, resource requirements, change control, and PM authority.

Collectively, these elements define the project scope, requirements and charter. Your organization may also require other narrative documents but the elements above are critical for controlling projects and achieving success. They are the strategic foundation for a successful project.

Technique #1 Defining the Project Scope

Scope: Measure of Success

An objectively verifiable business outcome
- Clarity on what the sponsor wants
- Scope change control
  - Clarifies what is included in the project
  - What is excluded because it's not necessary
- Clear team performance expectations

You need to drive projects from quantifiable scope definitions. Driving a project plan from the success measures keeps the focus where it should be; on achieving the end result. By working with the Customer to define success before the project

Construction Project Essentials

starts, the PM is in a much better position to control the project.

As an example, let's say the Director of Human Resources for a medium sized company, contacts you about doing a project. She says, "I know that this is not your specialty but you are the only project manager I know. I need your help. Our personnel records are so out-of-date that it takes us days to find out what department a person works in. On top of that, employees' quarterly performance reviews are useless, if they get them at all. I want you to remodel the space so we can straighten out that whole mess. When a line manager calls, we must be able to find up-to-date employee personnel records, both paper and electronic, so we can quickly give them the data they want. We need to be able to locate the employee reviews that give solid, detailed feedback on their performance. We need remodeling of our office space to make all this work smoothly."

You finished writing some notes, wishing you could stick with your kind of construction projects. Then the Human Resources Director went on, "You can use anyone you want to get this done. This is a high priority. You'll probably have to involve five or six people from our group, some line mangers and someone from Administration, IT, as well as Facilities/Construction so you get a lot of good input. Decide on how to organize the files, the space and what standards the performance reviews should meet. A good place to start is probably by updating all the records. Then maybe you can draft a memo, for my signature, telling managers that they have to do performance reviews on time and give their people useful feedback on their performance and developmental needs. You get the team, crews and subs put together and we will figure out the rest of the project from there."

Construction Project Essentials

The Human Resources Director has given you a lot of information about this project and what you're supposed to do. It would be very easy to start work on the file room and draft that memo. However, all of the information is in the form of activities. The Human Resources Director hasn't told you what end result she wants. To succeed with this project, you have to know how she is going to measure the success of the project when you're done. That definition will give you a tool to control the scope of the project and decide what should, and what should not, be included in the project work.

So, you have to ask the Human Resources Director some questions to get at the business purpose of the "laundry list" of changes that she talked about. You might start by asking, "After the files are up to date, the room is remodeled and the managers are doing thorough performance reviews on time for all the employees, what will that do for us?"

The Human Resources Director answers, "We'll be on top of things!"

You sense she is getting just a little bit angry at the questions but you press on because if you don't find out what problem she wants to solve and how she will measure success, you have almost no chance of delivering it. So you continue.

"If I know exactly what end result you want, I can do a good job and give you exactly what you want. So let me ask this, three months after we finish this project, what will be different; what will you expect to see?"

"Okay," the Human Resources Director sighs and then pauses for a moment to think. "Three months after the project's done, I won't have managers complaining to me that we don't know what's going on and how it takes forever to get employee information from us."

Now the Human Resources Director is talking about end results instead of activities so you know you're on the right track. But you have to change these end results into metrics, measurable achievements.

You ask, "So if I understand what you want, the employee records have to be current. How current? Would five days be good enough?"

She thinks for a moment and says, "No, we can do better than that. Let's say the files and records in the personnel system are never more than 3 days behind."

You make a note and then ask, "With the files and records current to within 3 days, how fast do we have to answer a line manager's questions about our people?"

"That's a hard one," the Human Resources Director says, frowning in thought. "Some complex data requests will take time- a day or two, others just a few seconds."

"Well, how about we set the goal at '80% of the requests are answered in 10 minutes or less'?"

The Human Resources Director grins and says, "How about 95%?"

You smile back and say, "It will take a lot longer to get that close to perfection. What percentage are we answering within 10 minutes now?"

She frowns again and says, "About 1%. Let's go with 80%; that'll be a great improvement."

Construction Project Essentials

What you've done in this planning session is to get agreement on the scope of the project. You now have an unambiguous scope defined with a metric. You have quantified the Human Resources Director's expectations for the project and you will use it to drive the planning process. . You've also given yourself a tool for controlling changes to the scope of the project. When the Human Resources Director was talking about objectives like "straightening up the records" and "being on top of things" it's very hard to decide what is, and what is not, a change in the scope. With a measurable deliverable to quantify your scope, controlling scope creep is much easier.

Activity Trap: Project Death Spiral

We focusing only on what to do next...
   not the outcomes we want at the end
◆ Activities are so easy to list, that we
   think are making progress
◆ A sound project plan is not a list of
   attractive features or good ideas

You avoided the activity trap in the discussion with the Customer, but it is such an obstacle to project success that we will delve into it in a bit more detail. The deadly lure of the activity trap defeats many efforts to clarify the scope of

Construction Project Essentials

projects during initial planning. This initial planning phase is the point at which a Project Manager (PM) and the Customer can easily fall into the activity trap. The Customer usually has a few ideas about features and the first several steps for you to do and then says, "It's time to get going on that project and start work immediately." That "start fast and plan later" approach is a project killer.

Why? Everyone has a list of good ideas and activities that can make it into a long "To Do" list. You can hope that these activities improve performance and hope the result satisfies the Customer. But there's entirely too much hoping going on here. In the activity trap, the project manager has no way to measure when the tasks are successfully completed. How does the PM decide what tasks to include or how much time and resources to invest in each of them? Politics and power alone will determine what's in the project and it will forever be a moving target.

The main problem is that none of the activities connects with a deliverable. Because the PM never asked the Customer to define success, the PM is in a situation where the Customer will define success as the project progresses or at its conclusion. Worse, the definition of success will be a moving target and the Customer will change it to move the effort in directions they favor.

The project manager and the Customer have fallen into the "activity trap." They'll add new activities each week rather than driving the project plan toward the scope. They buried themselves in the minutia of tasks rather than focusing on the end result. They added tasks to the plan because they sounded good or they had used them before. The project won't solve the business problem that triggered it.

Construction Project Essentials

Technique #2 Requirements & High-level Deliverable Network

The scope is not the last measured deliverable you'll develop, but it is the most important and the most difficult to conceive. With the Customer's approval of the scope, the project manager can begin decomposing it into high-level deliverables that lead to the scope. The high-level deliverables are not activities; they are also measured business results. You don't think about how you're going to do the work, you simply identify the major measured results which will carry you from where you are now to where you need to be; the project scope.

Let's continue with our example and see how you need to handle the development of the high-level deliverables for the personnel records project, using the scope the Human Resources Director has approved.

Sometimes, you'll sit down and lay out the requirements for a project yourself. Other times, you'll involve the project team, crews and subs in the process. Let's start by thinking it through, develop some requirements ideas and then show them to the team, crews and subs. To reach the project's scope, "80% of the info requests answered in 10 minutes," the Human Resources Director gave you a few ideas.

1. The records have to be current on all personnel actions.

2. Managers have to turn their quarterly performance reviews in on time

3. The performance reviews have to be thorough

Construction Project Essentials

4. HR staff has to know how to efficiently answer inquiries in the system.

With these ideas in mind, you might start talking to a number of other people, including line managers, HR staff, IT staff and the crews/subs, to flesh out the deliverables. Each of these discussions starts with you acquainting everybody with the project scope. These discussions are another opportunity to dive headfirst into the activity trap and all those delicious ideas. You keep the conversations on track by talking about end results. If people think the requirements make sense, then you work to convert them into measured deliverables.

Let's take one of the requirements, "The performance reviews have to be thorough," as an example. Now that is an activity and you'll have to convert it into a measured deliverable. That's your normal process. You think through the activity and then convert it into a measured deliverable. You might talk to some managers and find that they don't know what should be in a "thorough" performance review or how to do it. This gives you some ideas.

You talk to the Human Resources Director and get a list of 17 items that are required for a quarterly employee performance review. Another requirement is to train the managers on how to complete those reviews. From this thinking, you might come up with an end result like "95% of the quarterly performance reviews contain the 17 required items." That's your high-level deliverable, and to support it you'll need sub-deliverables for developing and getting approval of the standard. How do you measure that requirement? Maybe the management committee should approve the review standard. So you'll assign a team member to develop the performance review standards and that assignment will produce a

Construction Project Essentials

measured business outcome of "Management committee approves 17 item performance review standard."

You also need to train the managers in doing performance reviews that meet the standard. How do you measure training? You think through the purpose of the training, which is to increase the managers' competency in doing employee performance reviews. Then you think about how you will assess the training program you finish it. Last, you think about how you would measure if the training succeeded. You might decide that a test at the end of training is the best way to measure its effectiveness. That might lead to a deliverable of "90% of the managers score 80% or higher on a test of the performance review standards."

The thinking you've gone through is to gather ideas on your requirements then transform them into measured deliverables. You think about each activity and how you will assess the assignment when the team, crew member or sub finishes it. The criteria you will use in assessing the completed assignment becomes your measured deliverable. Conceiving measured deliverables is difficult for everybody because we are all so accustomed to activity lists. But the thinking investment leads to everyone knowing what you expect of them before they start work.

The completed high-level deliverable network, with the deliverables subdivided, is below. This is a very simple looking document, reflecting a great deal of thought. When the Customer approves this network, you can proceed with the rest of the plan.

Construction Project Essentials

Completed Deliverable Network

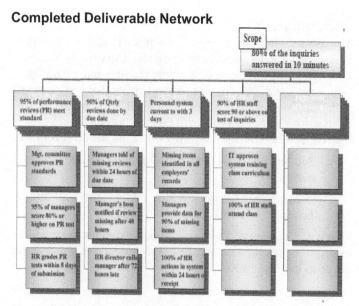

The graphic above shows the requirements for the project in deliverable network form. You'll use this deliverable network as the backbone of your project plan after the Customer has approved it.

With the scope and high-level deliverables defined, you can move on to the other components of your charter.

Construction Project Essentials

Technique #3 Charter: Problem Avoidance

The risk section of the Charter is the place to identify potential issues concerning resources and politics. Uncovering the assumptions underlying a deliverable requires some thought. Below are a few risks for your project. Note that you've stayed at the business results level and avoided those pointless assumptions like, "everyone will do their task on time." Instead, you have focused on what can cause the project to fail:

1. Building materials or crews/subs aren't available when needed.

2. Managers and their bosses don't do reviews that meet the approved standards.

That's it. You may add another one or two but the point here is to keep the list short so the risks to the project's success get the attention they deserve.

Assumptions, Constraints & Risks

- ◆ Risk assessment and avoidance
- ◆ Assumptions about customer or employee behavior and reactions
- ◆ Politics, conflict and messy turf issues
- ◆ Covers only the "show-stoppers" that threaten the MOS™

Construction Project Essentials

With the scope, a high-level network of deliverables and the risks, you can complete the plan by proposing to the Customer the authorities you will need to manage the project.

Authority, Resources & Change Control

- ◆ People we need
- ◆ Their availability
- ◆ Our authority to manage
  - Directly assign work to project team members
  - Evaluate performance
  - Reward performance
- ◆ Scope change control

It's time to do a little thinking on the resources you need and your authority to manage them. You'll use your deliverable network for this and it shows the deliverables you'll need from many other people. When you subdivide the high-level deliverables, you involve people from other organizational units who will produce some of the deliverables.

Now not all the project crew members work for you. Many may have the same boss but you don't have any formal authority to assign them work or evaluate their performance. They all have other jobs besides working on your project.

So your project charter aims at getting the Customer to help you secure the resource and the authority to manage them.

Construction Project Essentials

You'll want to avoid going to the Customer every time a team member, crew or sub's assignment is late. So you establish your authority now to avoid problems later.

You ask for the resources you need and the authority to manage them during the planning process because your chances of getting some level of authority are far better now than if you wait until you have a problem with a team member, crew or sub.

So in the charter for the example project, you'll ask for resources and authority. For a trainer named Jill, you might say, "I need approximately 50 hours of Jill's time during the next 60 days to develop and deliver the performance review training. Please adjust her workload to make these hours available and tell her that I will be assigning her work within that 50-hour block of time. Also, my evaluation of her work will be considered in her quarterly performance review." You may not always get that authority but it's worthwhile to ask for it.

Another part of the charter is your recommended procedure for controlling changes to the scope of the project. This process should include documentation of the requested change, analysis of the impact on scope, time, cost and resources, which the Customer accepts or rejects.

Construction Project Essentials

Broadbrush Plan Approval

- ◆ Scope – Measure of Success
- ◆ Requirements – Achievement network
- ◆ Charter
  - Assumptions, Constraints & Risks
  - Resources
  - Authorities
  - Change Control Mechanism
- ◆ Approval lets us start scheduling

Charter Plan Approval

With the preceding elements of the plan complete, you are ready for the first of your project presentations. At this first meeting, you're looking for the Customer to approve your charter & strategy for the project. Some Customers want a detailed schedule and a final commitment on the completion date at this first session. But you are far better off to get approval of the high-level plan and then develop the details. There are several reasons for taking this two-step approach:

First, putting a schedule together is a lot of work. You avoid redoing it by getting the Customer's approval on the scope and charter before you put the schedule together. Second, when you present a schedule people tend to dive into the details and you want some attention paid to the big picture. This session need not be a long meeting, particularly if you've been

showing the Customer the pieces as you finish them. But the
two-step approval process is the better way to do it.

Step Two: Work Breakdown Structure

With the charter approved, you can continue the top down
planning process with another level of decomposition, if
necessary. The charter provides you with an approved
network of deliverables, each of which ties to the project's
overall scope. If the assignments are too large, you can
decompose them further. This creates a work breakdown
structure (WBS).

Now, you're ready to dive into the software without
abandoning the idea of measured deliverables. You do not
write long laundry lists of every possible thing people can
think of. Instead of viewing the work breakdown structure as a
"To Do" list, you need to view it as a list of the deliverables
your team, subs and crews are accountable for producing.
That's how you'll manage the project and the assignments
within it. On 1-person projects, you can list all the activities
and be reasonably accurate in identifying everything you need
to do (i.e. planting your herb garden or a small remodel
project).

But when the projects get bigger, you want to build a small
project plan that is easy to keep current and which focuses on
the deliverables they are accountable for producing, not every
nit-picky sub-task.

Now, many Customers are accustomed to seeing monstrously
long and highly detailed work breakdown structures. It is not
unusual to see a 3-month project with 5 crews/subs have 400

or more lines in the work breakdown structure. While this may look impressive at the start, and may convince people that the PM is "really in control of what's going to happen," this is a fantasy.

What happens to these monstrously detailed work breakdown structures? They create project plans that are very time-consuming or impossible to maintain. In fact, so many of those detailed tasks change each week that it takes too much time to update the project plan, so the PM doesn't do it. This leaves them with no tool to manage the project. They may have impressed the Customer at the beginning with all the details but they cannot exercise control over what's happening, spot problems or fix them.

Even worse, these monstrously detailed work breakdown structures undermine the commitment and accountability of the crews and subs. If you assign the crews/subs a To Do list, that's all they take responsibility for completing. Without much thought, they complete the list of items on their To Do list, having no sense of responsibility for the deliverable that should result at the end of their work. Only the project manager is responsible for end results. This is another example of micro-management. You want project crews and subs to feel accountable for producing a business result and solving the problems they encounter along the way, not just completing a checklist.

You do have standard procedures to follow in many types of projects. But all the steps in a standard procedure shouldn't be in the project plan. You can craft a measured deliverable of completing the required 17 steps and leave the details in the procedure manual. Completing those 17 steps is important and part of the deliverable but why track each one?

Construction Project Essentials

Now, not every crew/sub can successfully complete a large deliverable that takes 10 days, without detailed instructions. For some crews and subs, assignments of two or three days are better. For others, small assignments will not engage their interest or commitment. As we will discuss later, you have to craft assignments that are the "right" size for each of the crews/subs on your project. But the answer is not to give every crew/sub a highly detailed To Do list of 1-day tasks.

You may be saying to yourself, "But they won't know what to do." Again, if you want them to follow a standard operating procedure in completing their assignments, as is often the case, then you should make adhering to the procedure part of the deliverable. But this does not mean that you must write the entire procedure into the work breakdown structure. As an example, if your organization has stress test procedures, you can assign an engineer to that deliverable stated as "meet all of the stress test requirements on page 26 of the procedure manual." You don't need to list all of those required steps.

In sum, you want to design the work breakdown structure as a listing of the deliverables you will hold crews and subs accountable for producing. This will give you a small project schedule which crews/subs will be able to look at and understand. As importantly, you will be able to update it in 10 or 15 minutes per week and always have the up-to-date version of the project schedule from which you can answer their questions. This approach is far better than developing a monstrous project plan, which may impress the Customer and crews/subs at the beginning but which proves useless in managing your project, reporting status or in developing solutions to the project's problems.

Now, let's discuss the project management software.

Construction Project Essentials

Technique #4 Using Project Software

How We Use the Software

- ◆ Not a spreadsheet or word processor
- ◆ It's a dynamic computer model of:
  - Task durations
  - Dependencies between tasks
  - The project's duration
- ◆ Every time we make a change it automatically optimizes the schedule to finish as early as possible

An effective method of learning is to enter the following project plans into the Microsoft Project® software.

We'll tackle the use of project software in the following sequence:

1. Develop the Work Breakdown Structure (WBS)

2. Create a predecessor network

3. Assign crews/subs and estimate work

4. Obtain schedule approval

5. Track actual results and solve problems.

Throughout this process, you'll use the software as a tool to manage the project, not to list all the micro-tasks in it. Accordingly, you'll create a work breakdown structure (WBS) of crews/subs' deliverables. Then you'll combine these with predecessor relationships between deliverables. Finally, you'll

Construction Project Essentials

assign crews/subs to the deliverables with an estimate of the
amount of work and let the software calculate the duration.
That calculated duration reflects the required hours of work
and the availability of your crews/subs to complete it. So
you'll start with a project plan that based on work estimates
and resource availability, not start and finish dates plucked out
of the air.

You may be used to entering start and finish dates. However,
resource-driven scheduling as outlined above is a far superior
technique. Whenever you have a change to the work or a
person's availability, the software will update the whole
schedule dynamically. We will talk later about making work
estimates and managing crews/subs' utilization.

Start Date

When you open Microsoft Project® or click {File} {New},
you see a blank project document. To set the start date of the
project, go to {Project} then {Project Information}. The only
date you'll enter is the start date of the project. The software
will calculate the finish date for you after you do your plan.
You usually want to finish a project as soon as possible so
leave the setting "Schedule from: Project Start Date" as it is on
the graphic. You'll also use the standard calendar for the
moment so leave that alone too. To get to this screen at any
time, click on {Project} then {Project Information}. From
here, you can click {Statistics} to get a summary of your
project.

For now, let's enter the start date, or our best guess about the
start date, and move on. You can always change the start date
later and setting it up this way will allow the whole plan to
adjust automatically.

Construction Project Essentials

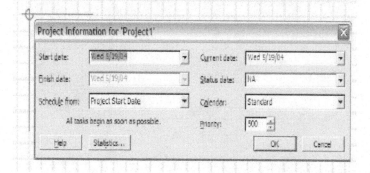

Construction Project Essentials

Summary & Subtasks

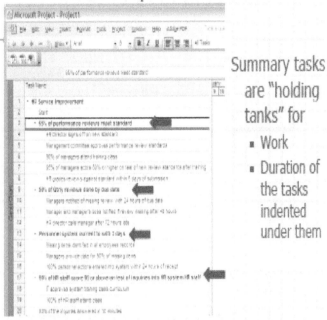

Summary tasks are "holding tanks" for

- Work
- Duration of the tasks indented under them

On the WBS, you have summary tasks with subtasks indented underneath them. The summary tasks are in bold. Summary tasks are holding tanks. You don't assign resources, enter work, durations, start/finish dates or predecessors to a summary task. When you move to tracking actuals, you'll enter completed work only for subtasks. The system rolls-up information from the subtasks and reports it for their summary task. This is easy to forget but summary tasks are the "subtotals" in our project plan. You'll use them for high-level reporting. Again, a summary task has subtasks under it. That's the definition.

In detailing your project network, there are no magic rules about how many tasks to have. A common error, as we've discussed, is to have too many. Planning with deliverables rather than activities, helps reduce the number of tasks. Think of tasks as important deliverables in the project that you wish to track.

Construction Project Essentials

Getting to Our Data Entry Screen

Setting the Task Entry View

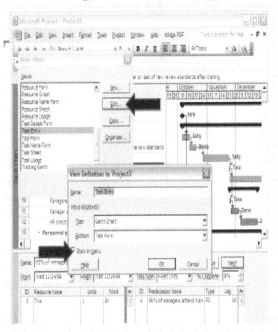

There are hundreds of ways to enter and display information in Microsoft Project®. You're going to use just one view for all your data entry. You get to that view by clicking {Views} {Gantt chart} {More Views} and going down the menu, as in the graphic, until you find {Task Entry}. Highlight it and then click {Edit}. Next, put a checkmark in the little box next to "Show in menu" and the task entry view will be on the drop down list under {View}.

Construction Project Essentials

The Task Entry Screen

The Task Entry screen is a split screen view. The upper part shows you the Gantt chart of the project. When you highlight a task on the WBS (row #7), you see the details of that task in the lower half of the window.

In the lower half, the left side shows whom you assigned to the task and the right side show the predecessors of that task. While this takes a bit of getting used to, the task entry view lets you do everything you need to set up a project schedule. You will also use it for tracking.

Construction Project Essentials

Task Entry Screen

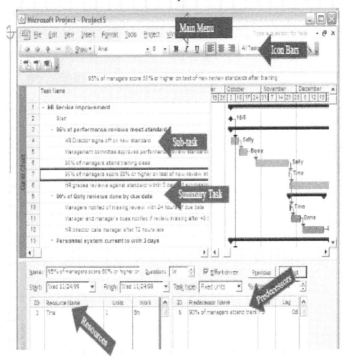

Technique #5 Decomposition of the Work Breakdown Structure

With the task entry view in place, you enter your high-level deliverables and their sub-deliverables in the "task name" column in the upper half of the screen. To give yourself easily accessible totals, the first line of the WBS should be the name of the project. You'll make this a summary task by indenting every other row in the project under it. Then all your reports will have the project totals on the first line.

On the second row of the WBS, enter a task called "Start." Later you'll give this task a zero duration making it a milestone. Every task that starts on the first day of the project will have "Start" as a predecessor. Use the right-

pointing arrow on the second row of the icon bar (see the arrow pointing to it), to indent "Start". Indenting "Start" also makes the task above it a summary task. On the third line, you'll enter your first high-level deliverable and use the right pointing arrow to indent it once, so it has the same indentation as "Start."

Next, you'll enter your sub-deliverables under the first high-level deliverable (HLD) and indent them one tab more. When you enter the second sub-deliverable, the software will continue the previous indentation. You'll continue and enter the rest of the sub-deliverables until you come to the second high-level deliverable. Now you have to "out dent" this HLD once, so that it matches the indentation of the first HLD and you do that with the left pointing arrow. You continue with the rest of the HLD's and sub-deliverables until you have entered the whole plan. The scope for the project is the last line of the plan. You indent it the same amount as a high-level deliverable but in small projects, it usually has no sub-deliverables under it. That's all there is to the data entry of the WBS.

Construction Project Essentials

WBS & Our Deliverables

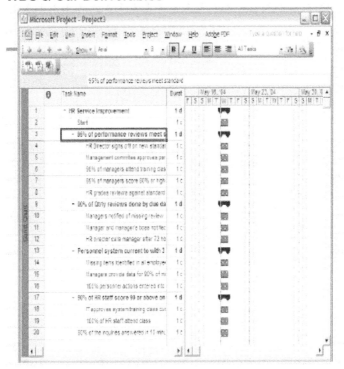

Here is the completed WBS for the Human Resources project example. Notice how all the task bars line up in a column. By default in the software, they all have a duration of one day and start on the start date of the project. You'll change this later as you build the plan.

Now this is a small project plan with 20 rows. It's easy to see what has to happen and it will be easy to update. Could you make it bigger? Sure, but you'll add more detail only when you need to add it to make assignments more clear.

Assignments & Micro-management

This work breakdown structure may be very different from what you see at work. It sets up the project manager to hold the project crews/subs accountable for end results, not all the steps in getting there. Is this project manager taking terrible risks? Not really. Project managers who hold project crews/subs accountable for their end results are PMs who get the most from the crews/subs working on the project. They trust people to a reasonable degree. Within the scope of the deliverable they have crafted for the crews and subs, the PM trusts them to deliver it. And remember, it is the PM who controls the "size" of the assignment and thus the degree to which each crew/sub will be trusted.

A micro-managing PM is just the opposite. This type of PM trusts no one and feels that he has to watch everybody closely because they will do the wrong thing if not monitored. Think back to micro-managing bosses you may have had. How much enthusiasm did you bring to the job? How much accountability did you feel for the end results? The answer to both questions is probably very little.

Micro-managing as a PM style also limits the number of crews/subs and the size of projects that a PM can manage successfully. The micro-management technique collapses when the crews/subs get bigger than 4-5 and/or when the micro-manager does not have more expertise than every crew/sub does. Micro-manage works when you know more about the work than the crews/subs doing it. If you don't, then the recipients of the micro-management get pretty resentful of that style. Again, think back to a time when you had a new boss who knew less about your job than you did. What was your reaction when this person tried to micro-manage you?

For all these reasons, consistently successful project managers are not micro-managers. Within the limits of each crews/subs' capability, successful project managers specify end results and leave it to the crews/subs to figure out how to get there. They get interesting benefits with this management approach. Crews and subs find work on the project more rewarding and they feel encouraged to use their creativity. This difference in the level of enthusiasm and commitment can be worth a great deal. You will avoid the pitfalls of micro-management when you design your work breakdown structure.

Step Three: Dynamic Schedules

Your next step is to take the WBS and add the predecessor relationships. It's important to remember that you specify only the immediate predecessors of a task. If task C cannot start until B finishes and task B can't start until A finishes, then task C's predecessor is B. and task B's predecessor is A. All you need to enter is that B is C's immediate predecessor and A is B's immediate predecessor. There are a number of types of predecessor relationships:

- Finish to start - A must be finished before B can start

- Finish to finish - A and B must finish at the same time

- Start to start - A and B must start at the same time

Construction Project Essentials

· Leads and Lags - any of the preceding predecessor relationships can have a time delay (lag) or time acceleration (lead).

Finish to start, lag 3 days, means task B can start 3 days after task A finishes. Let's look at each of these types and see how to enter them in the software.

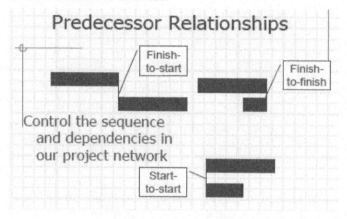

Technique # 6 Task Sequence

Task Sequencing

- ◆ Tell the software what the sequence of tasks has to be
- ◆ Task B can't start until A is finished
- ◆ Using predecessors is far faster than entering start and finish dates because the software automatically updates the plan for us and optimizes the schedule

You may be used to entering start and finish dates for each task in a project plan. All that does is make more work for you. You want the software to automatically adjust dates as things change. That's how you can limit your computer time to 10 minutes a week and keep everyone informed about what's going on.

So you will build your project schedule with predecessor relationships between the tasks. Then the software can calculate the start and finish dates for each task based on its predecessors, work, and resource availability. When you make a change to the schedule, the software will recalculate every start and finish date and instantly give you a revised schedule.

Entering Predecessors

Construction Project Essentials

To do your predecessor data entry you'll skip down to task 4 in the upper half of the window. Why skip? Because tasks 1 and 3 are summary tasks, you don't connect them to your network. Task 2 is Start; the first task in the project and it doesn't get a predecessor.

Task 4, "HR Director signs off on new standard" is a yes/no deliverable where you will develop a performance review standard and gain the Customer's approval. Work on this deliverable can start on the first day of the project so you will make its predecessor Task 2, Start, by entering a "2" in the ID column. Then click OK.

Predecessor Data Entry

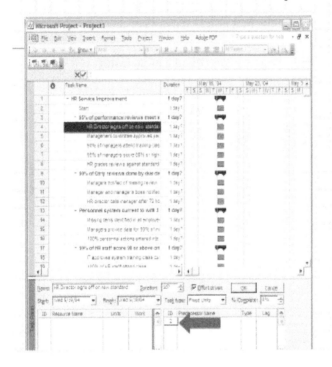

Our First Predecessor

You'll see that the software has done two things. In the lower
half of the screen, it has filled in the name of task #2 and put
FS (that means finish to start) in the Type column. In the
upper half of the screen, the software has drawn a predecessor

line between task 2 and 4 and it has pushed task 4 out, so it starts after 2 is finished. That's a finish to start predecessor.

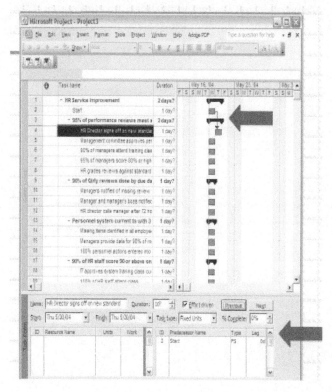

Finish-to-Start

As you look at the screen shot from Microsoft Project®, you see the work breakdown structure and Gantt chart with bars showing the start and finish dates for each task. The data entry screen in the lower half has a list of the predecessor

Construction Project Essentials

relationships on the right. This is the task entry screen in Microsoft Project® and you will use it for all of your data entry. Remember that you get to this view by clicking on {View}, {Gantt chart}, {More Views} and then select {Task}.

Entry Screen

The screen shot has task 5 selected in the upper half of the window. When you select it, the software frames it in black.

Construction Project Essentials

When you click on row 5 in the upper half of the window, you see the details of that task in the lower half. Looking at the Gantt chart, you see that task 5 starts right after task 4 finishes. In fact, you can see an arrow between the end of task 4 and the start of task 5. Looking at the lower right hand quadrant of the screen, you made that happen when you entered the predecessor as task 4 as a finish-to-start (FS) type. The way you create a finish to start predecessor is to click the task in the upper half of the window, then enter the number of its predecessor in the lower right hand quadrant. The software will fill in the name.

Finish-to-Finish

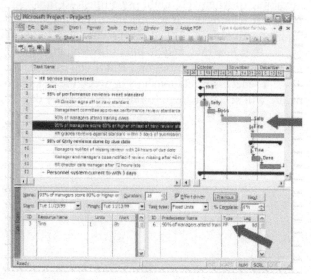

The next kind of predecessor relationship is finish-to-finish. When you click on task 7 in the upper half of the window, you see its details in the lower half of the screen. Task 6 is the predecessor of task 7 with a predecessor type of FF, finish-to-finish. You are telling the software that you want these two tasks to finish at the same time. In fact, you're telling the software that they **must** finish at the same time. When you create a finish-to-finish predecessor relationship between two tasks, like 6 and 7, the consequences can be serious. If something happens to postpone task 6, the software will also postpone task 7 so they will still finish at the same time. When you use finish-to-finish relationships you must be sure you mean it, because the software will schedule them that way unless the finish-to-finish relationship will result in an over allocation of recourses.

An example of when you might use a finish-to-finish predecessor relationship is the installation of a new system in various branch offices. This doesn't mean they'll all start at the same date because they may require different amounts of work and thus have different durations. But if you establish finish-to-finish predecessor relationships between the tasks, the software will schedule them to finish on the same day.

Construction Project Essentials

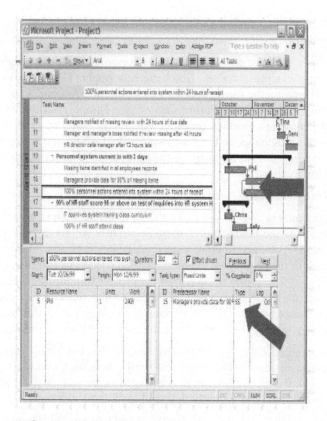

Start-to-Start

The last kind of predecessor is a start-to-start relationship. Here, you're telling the software that you want the tasks to start at the same time. The same warning as we discussed with finish-to-finish holds true. When you tell the software that you want the two tasks to start at the same time and something

Construction Project Essentials

happens to postpone the start of one, the software will postpone the other so they start at the same time.

An example of a start-to-start predecessor relationship might occur in a project where you have newspaper, TV and radio all advertising the same product. For marketing reasons, you might wish to have all three advertising campaigns running at the same time so they reinforce one another. In this case, if something happened to postpone the start of the newspaper ads you would want to postpone the radio and TV advertisements along with it.

Danglers in the Network

As you work your way down the work breakdown structure entering the predecessors, there is one rule you have to keep in mind. You need to close your predecessor network. Only one task in the project plan should have no successor and that is the scope. The scope is the end of the project so nothing comes after it. Every other task should have a successor. When your predecessor networks have more than one end, it can cause errors in the calculation of the duration of the entire project.

These are serious problems and so after you have built your predecessor network, and periodically thereafter, you will check the predecessor network to make sure you closed it and that the scope is the only deliverable with no successor.

As you look at the Gantt chart, you see that task 11 has no arrow coming out of the back end. That is, task 11 has no successor. In other words, task 11 is not the predecessor of any other task in the project. Task 11 is not the project scope so it's a dangler and you need to assign a successor (e.g. make it the predecessor of some other task). The Gantt chart is not the easiest place to spot danglers. Let's look at the network

Construction Project Essentials

diagram where it is a bit easier to spot them. You get to this chart by clicking {View} and then {Network Diagram}.

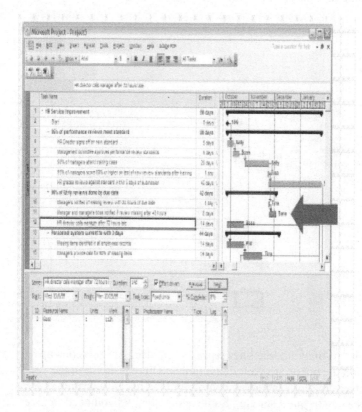

Network Diagram

Construction Project Essentials

To repeat, you need to have a closed predecessor network if you want the software to properly calculate the completion date of your project.

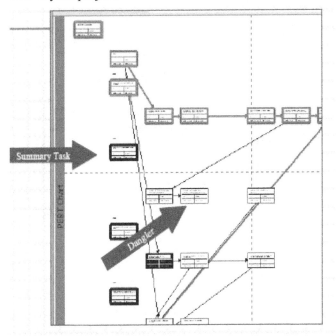

In this diagram, the lines represent predecessor relationships and the boxes are your deliverables. There is a task in the diagram that has no line coming out the back. It has no successor but it should. So it's a dangler and you need to give it a successor task. As a side note, the tasks with the shadows to the right and bottom are summary tasks and you should not connect them to the predecessor network.

When you add the missing successor task, you will have a closed network and only one end-point, the project scope.

Step Four: Assigning Resources to Tasks

Technique #7: Clear Assignments & Estimates

Now let's assign resources to tasks and estimate the amount of work required by their deliverable. There are many ways to enter resources. You'll use an easy one and you get to it by clicking on {Views}, then {More Views} and select {Task Entry} from the drop down list. Here's what you'll see. The upper half of the screen is your Gantt chart and the lower half shows the resources and predecessors of whatever task you clicked on in the upper half of the window.

You click on a task in the upper half of the window and see the details of the resources assigned to a task (lower left) and the predecessor relationships (lower right). Let's say you've decided to assign Sally the task of developing the performance review standards and securing the Customer's approval. Now, the key step in this process is to secure Sally's commitment to the deliverable and the work estimate. You'll hurt yourself and your project if you "ram" a work estimate" down Sally's throat and create a situation where she knows she will fail before she even starts work.

Construction Project Essentials

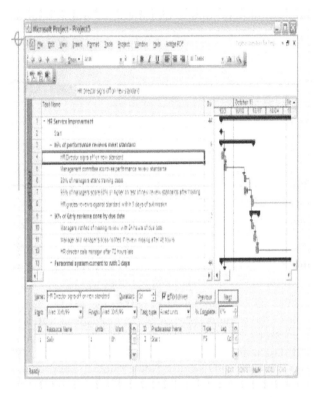

You'll discuss the assignment with Sally, after you secured her involvement and availability in your project charter. The assignment sounds like it should take about two weeks because she has to talk to a variety of people then draft a new standard for performance reviews. Next you'll review it with your Customer, the Human Resources Director, make any changes she suggests and get her approval. You could break this assignment into four or five smaller pieces but if Sally has done this kind of thing before, you'll give her the single, bigger deliverable. She tells you she thinks it will take 40 hours of work.

At this point, you need to set up your budgets and build estimates with your time. Let's first set up the resources. You right click on {Resources} then {Team Planner} and select resource sheet from the drop down list. You can set up all the resources at one time, entering their name, their max (maximum) units (1.0 is full time, 0.5 if half time) and their standard and overtime pay rates (if applicable). This makes assigning them to tasks easier.

You also need to work with your crews/subs to develop work estimates. Let them give you estimates that reflect the bad risks of the assignment, which would make it take more work and the good risks, which would take less work. You ask each crew/sub to give you 3 estimates: an optimistic estimate (only a 20% chance of the task taking less work), a

Construction Project Essentials

and the good risks, which would take less work. You ask each crew/sub to give you 3 estimates: an optimistic estimate (only a 20% chance of the task taking less work), a pessimistic estimate (only a 20% chance of the task taking more work) and a best guess estimate (a 50% chance of the estimate being too low). Then you enter those three numbers into the 3-point estimating tab for each task and the software calculates your work estimate at a variety of probabilities from 50% to 80% certainty. That lets you give the Customer a choice of certainty, recognizing that high certainty requires more work

Construction Project Essentials

and, thus, more cost. Remember that nothing is free in project management.

Name	Best	Pess	Opt	Mean	Standard Dev	Hours @50%	Cost @ 50%	Hours @ 70%
						Hrs	$	Hrs
85% of employees retrieve supplies in less than 2 minutes								
Start								
Sponsor approves design, plan & budget								
1-1: Managers approve storage design & ordering procedure	44	87	20	47.17	11.17	47	1651	53
1-2: Building department approves construction drawings	56	76	33	55.50	7.17	56	1943	59
1-3: Customer approves plans	8	10	5	7.83	0.83	8	274	8
1-4:		0	0	0.00	0.00	0	0	0

Construction Project Essentials

First Assignment

When you have Sally's agreement on the deliverable & the amount of work required, you enter the work number in the work column in the lower half of the screen on the left hand side. You enter the work as 40 and the software assumes hours. Then you type Sally's name in the Resource Name column and then click OK.

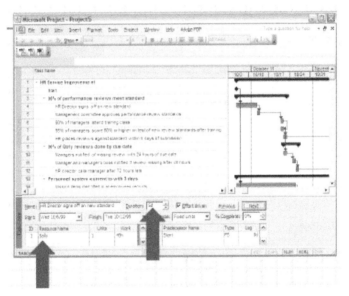

After you clicked OK, the software did several things. First, it filled in some additional data in the lower left hand quadrant of the screen. Second, it changed the Gantt chart and increased the length of the bar for task 4. It also pushed out the start date for task 5, which is a successor of task 4. What the software did was recognize the predecessor relationship you had established between the finish of task 4 and the start of task 5.

Construction Project Essentials

Because you told the software that task 5 could not start until task 4 had finished, the software used the duration it calculated to adjust the finish date of task 4. Then it adjusted the remainder of the project plan to reflect this information. Using this automatic updating of the project plan is much easier than having to adjust every start and finish date every time the duration estimates change. Last, the software put Sally's name on the Gantt chart so you know at a glance who's doing the work.

One standard in project management is that you discuss the duration of a task in terms of the number of working days that the task will take. You do not count weekends and holidays. You'll notice that Sally's task has a duration of five days but it starts on October 7 and finishes on October 13. That's seven days. However, looking at the Gantt chart you see that a weekend falls in the middle of Sally's assignment and that's why the calendar time is two days longer than the duration. This actually turns out to be very convenient because the duration of a task does not change due to weekends or holidays.

Second Assignment

The next assignment in the work breakdown structure is "Management committee approves performance review standards." You're going to assign this task to the Customer who will present the proposed standard to the management committee and secure their approval. You need to discuss this assignment with the Customer and secure their estimate of the duration it will take to get the management committee's approval.

Construction Project Essentials

Let's say the Customer tells you it will take five days duration to secure that approval. So, you'll type 40 into the work field, type "Boss" into the resource name field and click OK.

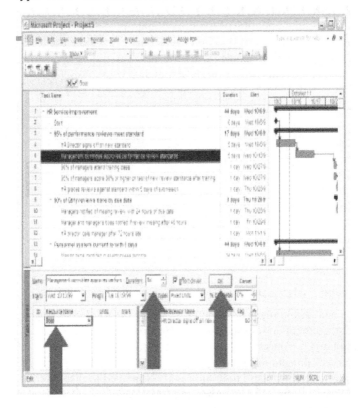

Third Assignment

Now let's go to task 6. You want to assign Sally to this task and so you will click into the resource name field and then single

Construction Project Essentials

click on the arrow that comes up to the right. It shows us a list of the resources you have used so far in the project. You want to be careful not to use two different names for the same crew/sub because the software will think you have two different crews/subs involved when, in fact, there is only one. To avoid making this mistake after you've entered the first couple of assignments, you'll always click on the arrow to get the drop-down list and then click on the crew/sub you want to assign. To finish, you'll select Sally, enter the work and click OK.

More on the Third Assignment

You may have noted that every time you made a change in the duration of a task in the lower half of the task entry screen, the software also made adjustments to the units and work columns in the lower left-hand side. The software calculates the number of full time equivalents it will take to do the work within the indicated duration. In the screenshot to the left, you see you have one full time person, Sally, doing 160 hours of work, which the software calculates, will take 20 days.

Construction Project Essentials

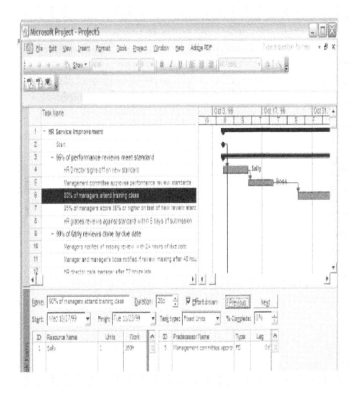

You got this result by entering 160 hours and assigning Sally to the task at the default unit, 1.0, which means she is working full-time. If she were going to work on this task halftime, you would assign her at .5 units or 50% of a full-time person.

You can assign resources to a task, enter the work and the software will calculate the duration. But when you look at the screenshot, you see that you're starting to run out of room to

Construction Project Essentials

see the whole project as the project's overall duration increases.

Adjusting the Time Scale

You can adjust the time scale on the Gantt chart in two ways. First, you can click into the upper half of the window and then click on the "zoom out "icon (magnifying glass with a minus sign). After clicking, you'll note that the view switched from a Gantt chart that shows every day to a Gantt chart that shows every three days. By changing to a larger time scale, you can see more of the Gantt chart. If you continue to click on the zoom out icon, the Gantt chart scale will change to weeks, then months, then quarters and so on. You can also zoom in to see smaller units of time, by clicking on the zoom in icon, which looks like a magnifying glass with a plus sign in it.

Construction Project Essentials

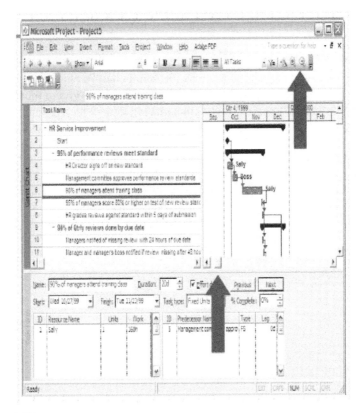

Milestones

You can proceed to assign work and resources to the rest of your tasks just as you've done for the first three assignments. There is another kind of task you want to have on the Gantt chart and that is a milestone. You make a task a milestone by entering zero in the duration field. This means that the task takes no calendar time and the software changes the symbol

Construction Project Essentials

from a bar to a diamond, as you can see on the illustration for the task "Start". "Start" is a good example of a milestone but you don't want use too many of them since every line in our plan is a measured deliverable. A good use of milestones is to mark important dates that won't change, like the end of a warranty period or a stockholder's meeting. For these, and only these milestone tasks, you'll enter a start date. But you won't make them part of your predecessor network. You don't enter start dates for your other tasks because that will "lock-up" the predecessor network and prevent the automatic schedule updating you want.

Construction Project Essentials

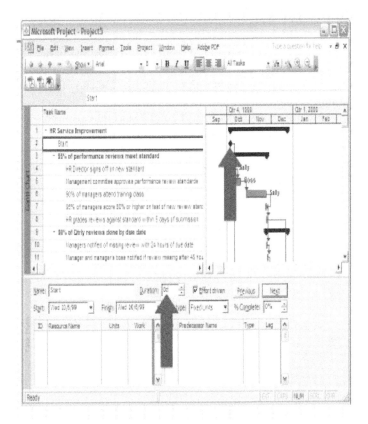

Completed Gantt Chart

After you've completed the rest of your assignments and
duration estimates, your project plan looks like this illustration.
You're getting close to the end and there are just a few
additional adjustments you have to make before you can
review the schedule with the Customer.

Construction Project Essentials

Before you move on, you can see that your project has several
paths. All of them end with task 20, your scope. But looking
at the Gantt you can see that three tasks have "Start" as a
predecessor and these paths then go to tasks 4, 14 and 18.
Another way of saying this is that you have parallel paths in
your project plan. This is good because it means that a number
of things are happening at the same time. The project will be
able to finish sooner than if only one thing was happening at a
time. Later you'll use these parallel paths.

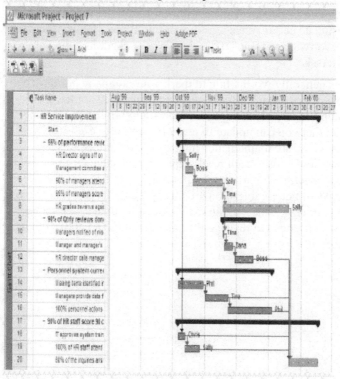

Construction Project Essentials

Scheduling and Calendars

You've been using the standard calendar that is the default in Microsoft Project®. On that calendar, you have scheduled no work for Saturdays and Sundays. You can refine the standard workweek definition by modifying the base calendar to prohibit the software from scheduling work on holidays and other non-working days so that your project duration is realistic. To adjust the calendar for your holidays, click {Project} then {Change Working Time} and you'll see the following calendar. You can move through the year and designate certain days as non-working time, which will cause the software to "skip" those days when scheduling the duration of a task.

It is generally worthwhile to mark your company holidays as non-working days. But it's easy to overuse customized calendars. Remember you are looking to build a small project plan that you can update in just a few minutes each week. Calendars are maintenance intensive and there is no sense spending 3 hours each week adjusting the calendar to reflect 1-hour meetings. The issue is granularity, or the size of the hunks of deliverables you are managing in the project. If most of your crews/subs' assignments are more than a week long, you don't need to manage the calendar at the level of 1-hour meetings.

Construction Project Essentials

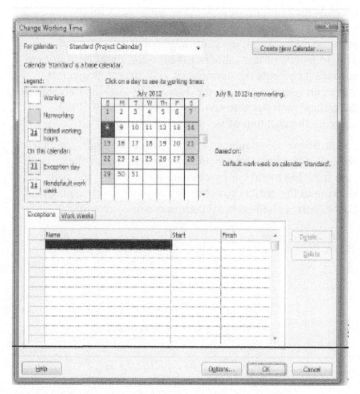

If, however, you are a real micro-manager and your assignments are at the level of 4 hours' worth of work, then prepare yourself for hours of calendar maintenance.

Technique #8 Critical Path

After you've adjusted the schedule for non-working days, you'll use the classic project management tool called the critical path. The critical path is the sequence of tasks that

Construction Project Essentials

controls the duration of your entire project. A few pages back you looked at your Gantt chart and saw that your project had multiple paths. The longest of these paths is the critical path. This sequence of tasks that has the longest duration is critical because it controls the duration of your overall project. It makes no sense to shorten the duration of tasks that are not on the critical path because shortening those tasks will not decrease the duration of the project as a whole.

The software calculates the critical path every time you make a change in your project schedule. You can display the critical path from the menu bar by clicking on {format} and then clicking in the critical path box. The system then displays the Gantt chart with the critical path in red on your screen.

.

©Copyright 2018 Dick Billows All Rights Reserved. May not be reproduced in any form without written permission

Construction Project Essentials

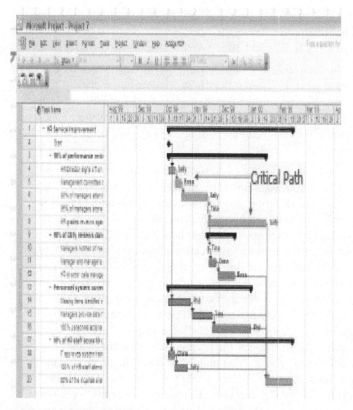

The Critical Path

The critical path is an important tool for project managers because you'll use it to shorten the duration of the project and finish earlier. Because shortening the duration is an issue on almost every project, you'll use the critical path frequently. As a reminder, it's called the critical path because it's the longest sequence of deliverables through the predecessor network of tasks. The critical path controls the duration of the project. The illustration shows the critical path in red. It begins on task 4, then 5, 6, 7, 8 and 20.

If the Customer wants a shorter duration, as is usually the case, you'll work to shorten the duration of only the critical path tasks. Shortening the duration of non-critical path tasks does no good in terms of shortening the project duration. So adding resources to non-critical path tasks is a waste of those resources.

If the Customer wants you to finish this project sooner, what task will you work on? The answer is task 8 because that is the longest duration task on the critical path and, thus, it is usually the best place to start. You scheduled Task 8, "HR grades reviews against the standard within 5 days" for about two months. That duration estimate was probably set to allow you enough time to give every manager feedback on the new performance reviews. How can you shorten it? You might suggest to the Customer that you change the project plan and require that every manager do a performance review on all his/her employees within 2 weeks following the training session. Then HR could check the reviews and give feedback in 4 weeks instead of 8. You may have other ideas on how to shorten this task. The one thing you should not do is just arbitrarily cut the duration. Remember you have a crew/sub who made a commitment to finish that deliverable in 8 weeks. You will lose that commitment if you don't adjust the deliverable to realistically allow them to finish in a shorter duration.

Will cutting the duration of this task shorten the project by 4 weeks? It depends. It is possible that not all of the task reduction will ripple all the way through to the project end date. You may find that cutting the duration of task #8 takes it off the critical path. Then you might find that while you cut the duration of task #8 by 4 weeks, the project's duration is reduced by only 2 weeks.

Before you go to the Customer for final approval, you should look for opportunities to shorten the duration by altering deliverables or adding resources to tasks on the critical path. Then you'll have an answer and a trade-off when the Customer asks, "How can we finish sooner?"

Final Review & Approval

During your final review session, you will present both the approved" project scope and charter as well as the detailed schedule and budget. You present both so no one forgets that the project schedule is dependent on the scope, assumptions, resources and authorities described in the charter. When you present both everybody remembers the linkages between these parts of your project plan.

You don't want to go into the final approval meeting with a mindset of "fighting for your project plan." Instead, you welcome changes but handle them as tradeoffs between scope, budget and duration. The trade-off for finishing earlier is either reducing the scope or using more resources. You'll talk about your willingness to make these trades but you're always clear that every trade has two sides. You might say, "If you take away two of my crews/subs, the project will finish 3 weeks later. If you want to increase the scope, the project will take longer and cost more."

Construction Project Essentials

◆ The project is prepared with:
- Scope
- Charter
- The schedule & resource assignments

◆ Boss always says it takes too long
- Have duration trade-offs ready
- Scope control starts during the approval meeting
- Maintain the team's commitments

In summary, you are not fighting because the Customer outranks or has hired (and can fire) you so you won't win the fight. Rather, you present the hard data upon which you have built your project plan. You agree to make any change they want as long as they understand that every change involves a trade. This approach is the way you can deliver on your project promises.

Construction Project Essentials

Technique #9 Leadership

Leadership begins very early during planning and continues throughout the entire life of the project. We'll talk about it here not because it's a last-minute kind of thing but because the project planning and scheduling you've now completed are the foundation upon which you will lead your crews/subs. The foundation you've built solves many of the problems that projects face. With your project scope and high-level deliverable network in place, you are in a good position to control the project's scope. You can avoid the typical problems project managers have trying to maintain the focus on measured deliverables. You're able to make assignments to your crews/subs that tell them what you expect before they start work. This part of the foundation saves them from having to guess about what's expected. As importantly, they don't have to worry about being "blind-sided" by requirements that change at the last minute.

You have also created a situation where you can develop a reasonable degree of the crews/subs' commitment to the project and their assignments. You don't gain this commitment by telling them they're committed to a due date. You gain commitment by negotiating with each crew and sub about the deliverable you need them to produce and the hours of work it will take. In the preceding steps, you developed estimates with your crews/subs rather than imposing them. You've also designed assignments that are important deliverables in the project, not long laundry lists of micro-tasks. Thus, to the limits of their capability, you trust your crews/subs to produce deliverables within the time frame you've negotiated. The project manager who trusts crews/subs certainly takes a risk. However, taking that risk and holding them accountable for

Construction Project Essentials

end results is an important part of the process of gaining their commitment to the project.

You'll use your project plan and schedule to inform every crew/sub about the project purpose and how their assignment contributes to achieving that end result. As you move into the tracking portion, you'll continue to give them information about how the project is doing and about changes to their assignments in the overall project schedule.

The typical situation for your crews/subs is that they are involved in multiple projects. The simple steps we've outlined here go a long way toward creating a trusting environment where there is little guessing and very little uncertainty about what's expected of them You can certainly add to that foundation with team building exercises and other "morale building" activities. However, when crews/subs can't find time to do all their project work, demanding extra time for these kinds of activities is a burden. It's far better to give every crew/sub clarity on your expectations and trust them to be accountable for their deliverables. That's much better than spending hours on team building activities followed by micro-management.

In addition to using your foundation properly, your leadership style with the crews/subs has an important impact on the culture of the project. The most common types of leadership and their general pros and cons are:

Autocratic – makes unilateral decisions for every crew/sub on the project without their input. This style takes little time but does not give the PM the benefit of the crews/subs' expertise.

Coaching – guides crews/subs to the correct decisions and processes. This style is time consuming but yields the benefit of enhancing the crews/subs' capabilities.

Construction Project Essentials

Consensus – builds agreement on actions using the inputs of the crews/subs. This style is very time consuming but is powerful when the crews/subs are experts in various disciplines, possess more expertise in their area than the PM, but must all come to an agreement.

Consultative – gathers inputs from the crews/subs prior to making the decision. This also requires more time than the unilateral styles but it is a powerful technique for building support from crews/subs.

Directing – gives instructions on what to do and is an efficient style that is most appropriate for emergency situations, but it does not build crews/subs' commitment.

There is no one style that is suitable for every PM in all situations. Project managers use many of these styles in different situations and with different crews/subs. Keep in mind that trying to use a style with which you are uncomfortable is never a wise choice.

Project Culture & Conflict
Every project develops a unique culture as the crews/subs work together. Sometimes that culture encourages bickering and blaming others for problems and failures. Other times the culture may encourage strict compliance with the rules and discourage creativity and innovation. Finally, other cultures encourage a strong achievement orientation with innovation and creativity to reach deliverables.

Construction Project Essentials

Team Culture & Conflict

- ◆ Culture of the team impacts:
  - Work attitudes (quality & productivity)
  - Commitment to assignment
- ◆ Assignments & reward style
  - Trust is reciprocated
  - Non-monetary rewards
  - Consistency in treating team performance

In every project culture, conflict will exist. You should not avoid conflict. Rather, you should directly address it with problem solving behavior that you aim at the causes. You should also involve the crews/subs having the conflict. You can handle conflict by using several techniques, including:

Compromise – developing a solution on which all crews/subs can agree. While this can bring temporary solutions, the conflict may revive.

Confronting – directly addressing the problem by unearthing the causes of conflict and addressing them with the crews/subs having the conflict. This style is the preferred style because it can lead to permanent solutions.

Forcing – This involves the use of power, authority or influence to impose a solution. This style often leads to continuing resentment and may not yield a permanent solution.

Smoothing – addressing the points of similarity rather than those of contention. This style minimizes the conflict while

Construction Project Essentials

emphasizing the points of agreement. It is usually a short-term solution.

Withdrawal – avoiding the problem by backing away from the conflict situation. This style also does not offer a permanent solution.

While every crew/sub influences the culture, the project manager's style is of paramount importance. Specifically, how you make assignments and what behavior you reward have an important impact on the overall project culture. If you make assignments to crews/subs with a style that shows you don't trust them and have no confidence in their ability to perform, it should not come as a surprise that they feel no sense of accountability for their project work. When you don't hold crews/subs accountable for solving at least some of the problems they encounter, you shouldn't be surprised when they bring every problem to you for resolution.

Project managers usually don't have monetary rewards to hand out to project crews/subs for successful completion of assignments. But this does not mean that you don't have any rewards whatsoever. You always have the option of buying lunch for a crew or sub who completes an assignment early or achieves more than you asked. But even if you don't have the budget to buy lunch, you still have a very powerful reward in our public praise of high achievers. And you can make lunch or your praise worth something to your crews/subs if you're careful about how you use it. If you praise everybody all the time, your praise quickly becomes valueless. Why is it valueless? Because the crews/subs know they have done nothing to earn it. If, on the other hand, you consistently praise those who finish on time or finish early but you don't give public praise for trying hard or having a good excuse, then you make your praise valuable. Because you usually have no other formal reward beyond that lunch or your public praise, it's important to maintain its value.

While you never want to criticize a crew or sub publicly, it is okay not to praise everyone. Thus, if two of crews/subs have finished early and three are late on their assignments, you will publicly praise the two who have finished early and say nothing publicly about the other three. This approach can be difficult to implement if you're concerned about causing embarrassment or bad blood. But if you praise crews/subs just so they won't be embarrassed or angry, your praise is soon worth nothing.

In summary, the way you manage the crews/subs in terms of assignments and rewards is a primary determinant of the project culture. One of the most difficult things about project management is to maintain a consistent style with the crews/subs when things are going badly. Yet a good project manager insulates the crews/subs from the Customer's displeasure by allowing those who have delivered their assignments on time to feel successful, even if there are problems with other parts of the project.

Step Five: Tracking Results

After all the work you've invested in setting up a project plan and establishing a schedule and budget, it's time to use that foundation to actually manage your project. Microsoft Project® software provides a number of analytical tools for tracking progress. The hardest part is often getting the status information from your crews/subs. They often less than diligent about submitting progress reports. But without them, a project manager is flying blind. It's never too early to make it clear how important progress reports are and how you're more than willing to adopt extreme measures (nagging, flogging, assault & battery) to receive them on time. You can also make it easier for them by the way you've built your plan. You need just the following numbers for each in-process task:

- % Completed
- Actual work completed
- Work Remaining.

Most projects are worthy of weekly progress reports from the crews/subs working on all in-process tasks. With data available on this frequency, you'll avoid nasty surprises at the end.

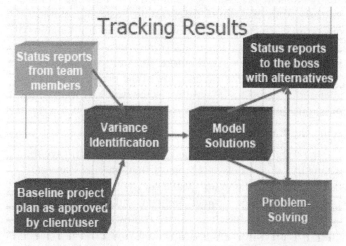

You'll also position yourself to solve small problems early rather than big problems late. By having status data updated and available weekly, you're able to take corrective action early and to "keep your hands off" tasks and crews/subs that are doing well. Constantly checking progress can quickly transform your style into micro-management.

The first step is to "save the baseline" by storing the approved budget and schedule so you can compare your actual results to it. Remember that every time you enter actuals, the system will change the task start and finish dates based on what has happened to each task and its predecessors. Having a stored copy of the original plan is the basis for your tracking analysis.

Technique #10 Tracking Actuals vs. Baseline

Your first step after the Customer has approved the plan is to save the baseline and preserve your ability to compare what's actually happened to what you planned. The baseline includes every task, start date, finish date, resource assignment and work estimate in the project. You can save several versions of the baseline, but you'll usually save just one. With this "snapshot" of the plan saved before you start work, you're set up to track progress for the duration of the project. Comparing actual performance to the baseline is the best way to develop your status reports.

Saving the Baseline

After the Customer has approved the project, you'll save the baseline like this: Click on {Project} then on {Set Baseline}. A new window will pop up. Make sure you fill in the "Save Baseline" and "Entire Project" buttons, and then click OK. You have saved the baseline. There is now a "Polaroid picture" of your entire project saved on your PC. As you enter changes and actuals, this baseline version of the plan will not change so you can always compare this original plan to your current schedule.

Construction Project Essentials

Creating the Baseline

◆ The baseline is our basis of comparison between actuals and every (date, task and predecessor the sponsor approved

◆ Tracking is very date sensitive so we need to record actual status on the "as of" date of the status reports

Status Reports

Before you enter status data, you need to tell the system the date your crews/subs submitted their status reports. Click {project} then "status date" and enter the "as of" date of the reports.

Let's jump ahead in time to the end of the first week of work on your project. You have three tasks that should have started. With a little nagging, you get all three status reports almost on time. Even though the status reports were due on Friday 10/8, you have them all by Monday morning 10/11.

You have status data on tasks 4, 14 and 18, all of which started on the first day of the project. So you'll click on task 4 in the upper half of the window to select it in the upper half of the task entry window you have been using. Click into the lower half of the window and then right-click and select "Work" from the drop down list. You see the display below. Sally tells you she has completed 45 hours of work on her task and that

Construction Project Essentials

she has 15 hours remaining. You can enter data into any two
of the three fields and let the software calculate the third when
you click OK.

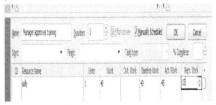

The software has stored the baseline data that the Customer
approved. It had Sally assigned full time with 40 hours of
work.

You see that Sally has already worked 45 hours and estimates
15 more for a total of 60. That is 20 hours more than the
baseline so you have a variance on this task.

Construction Project Essentials

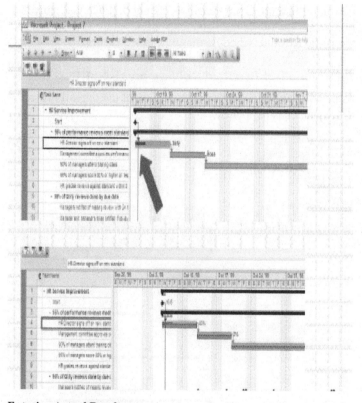

Entering Actual Results

In the upper screen shot, you see Sally's status report on the regular Gantt chart. Inside the Gantt bar, you see a darker progress bar that shows you how far along she is.

A better way to look at actuals is with the tracking Gantt shown in the lower screen shot. If you click on {Gantt chart} and select the {Tracking Gantt} from the drop down menu,

Construction Project Essentials

you'll see that the Gantt chart has changed. Each task now has two bars. The upper bar is the current schedule and the lower bar is the baseline schedule that you saved earlier.

Technique #11 Problem Solving and Reporting

After you have entered all the data, look at the overall project to see what has happened.

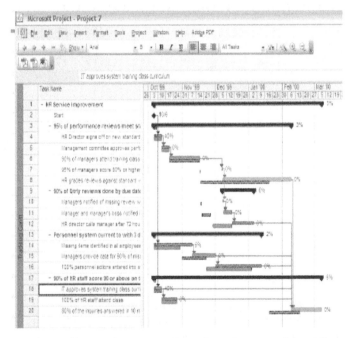

You have slippage in your project plan whenever the top bar (actual) is not aligned with the grey bar (baseline). Note the variance on task #8. That task started later than you planned in the baseline and will finish later too, if you don't take action.

Construction Project Essentials

Also, note how the slippage on task#8 and the slippage on task #14 have caused their successor tasks to have variances as well. The variance has rippled all the way through the project down to the scope and it's now showing that you will finish two weeks late.

Before starting your analysis, you need to update the schedule. Click on {Project} and {Update Schedule} and then select the option to "reschedule uncompleted work to start after." Then enter the date of the status report as shown below.

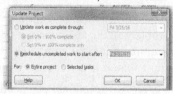

You should give the Customer and the crews/subs a printed copy of the tracking Gantt each week. That way they know the challenges the project faces. However, it is important to recall that these are the variances that will occur in the future if you take no action.

While some people may think it sounds good to "crack down hard on every variance," good project managers know that duration estimates can be wrong and that crews/subs do encounter unexpected problems. You need to focus your problem solving on real problems that affect the project completion date. As an example, it would be foolish to demand that all crews and subs work overtime to catch up on the slippage. That would waste time and money and have little impact on the project.

Where is the best place to solve the problem? The tendency is to think that you need to take action on the slipping tasks by committing more resources. But adding crews/subs to in-progress tasks doesn't always work. The new people have to be "brought up to speed" and that takes time away from doing the job. You may also find that two crews/subs can't efficiently do some tasks. Last, it is hard to find additional crews/subs who can start work immediately.

On the other hand, you might be able to recapture the earlier slippage by adding crews/subs to task 15, task 16 or to both. PMs tend to forget the "downstream" solution, thinking that it is vital to fix the problem in the task where it occurred. Yet it is often easier to acquire additional crews/subs starting two or three weeks from now than it is to get them tomorrow.

If you adopt these latter two solutions, you need to propose that corrective action to the Customer and get their help in securing the additional crews/subs. You'll also need the Customer's concurrence with the fact that you will be running behind the plan for several weeks until you reach the "catch up" task.

You'll go through this tracking, problem identification, resolution and reporting process each week for the duration of the project.

Construction Project Essentials

Technique #12 Closing the Project, Making the Next One Easier

When the project is complete, the project results have been accepted and verified by the Customer and you've completed your documentation, it is still valuable to close out the project with a "lessons learned" analysis. The point of this analysis is not to revisit every duration overrun in the project. Rather, you want to discuss how well the process of project management worked. During the lessons learned analysis, you'll spend most of your time on the project planning process and try to link problems you've had during the project to issues in your planning process.

Project Closing & Archiving

◆Project acceptance: Result verification

◆Lessons learned

◆Ideas for future projects

◆Focus on front-end processes:
- Scope
- Requirements
- Charter & Authorities

◆Archive data on how long tasks took to make estimating easier next time

It's easy to blame every overrun on bad crews/subs. But the fact of the matter is that you help yourself improve by making sure that your process of managing the project did not contribute to the overrun. You'll examine the clarity of the assignments you gave to the crews and subs, making sure they really could understand what they were supposed to deliver. You'll examine how well your project charter and its authorities worked. Were crews/subs pulled off the project despite the agreements you had about time commitments? Were the work estimates you used in the project schedule reasonable or did you fail to consider the complexity of some of the assignments? Were you able to control the changes the Customer made to the project? Did the mechanisms you put in place to limit "scope creep" work effectively?

The answers to these questions are the heart of your lessons learned. You may review these lessons with the Customer in the hope of making future projects more successful. You may also retain the information so that the next time you develop a project scope and schedule, you can use these examples of problems to make them better.

Another important issue in closing a project is to save the data on each of the tasks; the original estimates and the actual results in terms of how long and how much work it actually took to get the tasks done. This data is invaluable when you are doing estimating for your next project. It doesn't take many months before you have an estimating database that allows you to look for similar tasks and use the actual data as a starting point for your next estimating process.

Construction Project Essentials

Slide 1

Slides for Visual Learning Review

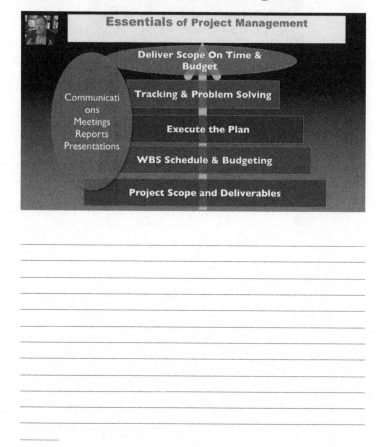

_____
_____
_____
_____
_____
_____
_____
_____
_____
_____
_____
_____
_____
_____

Slide 2

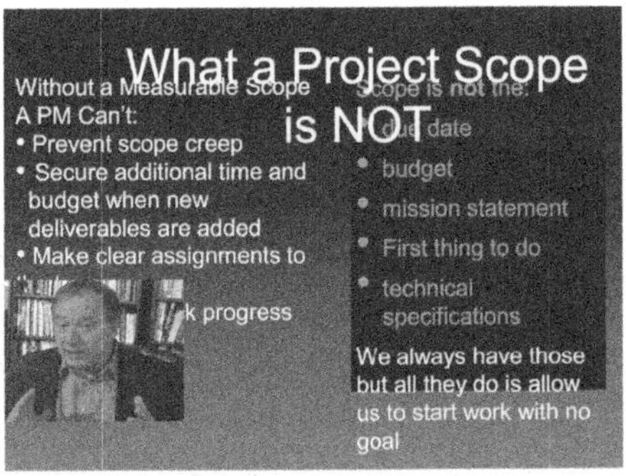
What a Project Scope is NOT
Without a Measurable Scope
A PM Can't:
• Prevent scope creep
• Secure additional time and budget when new deliverables are added
• Make clear assignments to
k progress
Scope is not the:
date
budget
mission statement
First thing to do
technical specifications
We always have those but all they do is allow us to start work with no goal

Construction Project Essentials

Slide 4

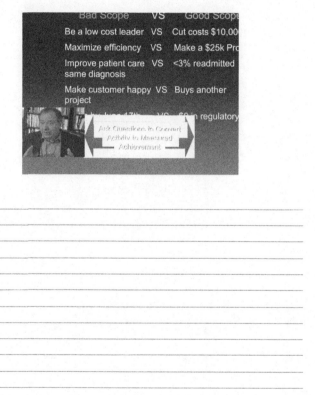

_____
_____
_____
_____
_____
_____
_____
_____
_____
_____
_____
_____
_____
_____

Construction Project Essentials

Slide 5

Construction Project Essentials

Slide 6

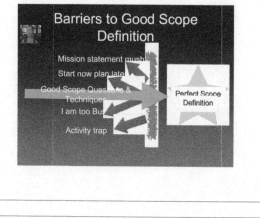

Construction Project Essentials

Slide 8

Construction Project Essentials

Slide 9

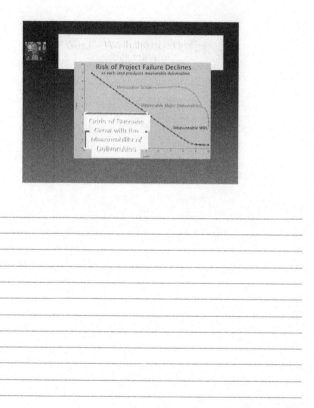

_____
_____
_____
_____
_____
_____
_____
_____
_____
_____
_____
_____
_____
_____
_____

Construction Project Essentials

Slide 10

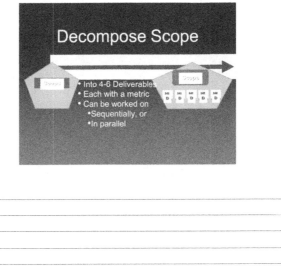

Construction Project Essentials

Slide 11

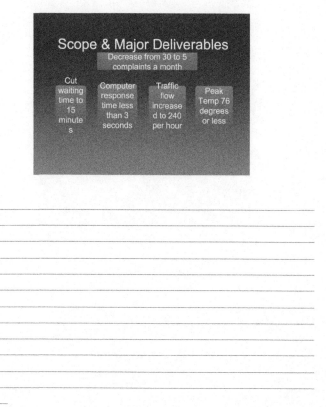

Construction Project Essentials

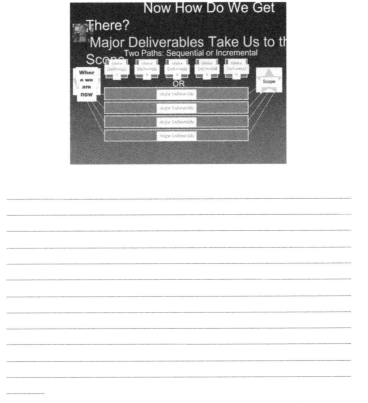

Slide 13

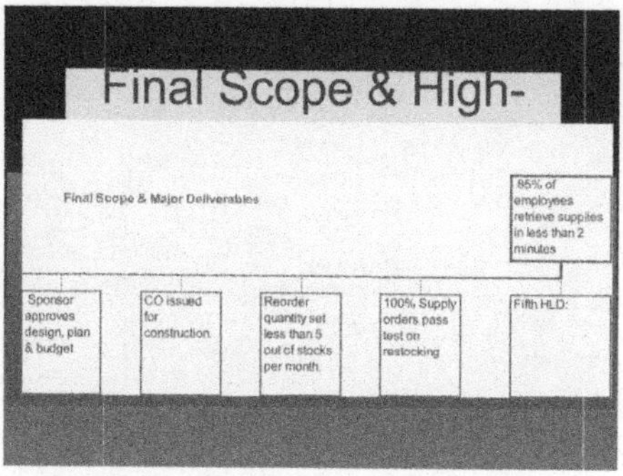
Final Scope & High-
Final Scope & Major Deliverables
85% of employees retrieve suppiles in less than 2 minutes
Sponsor approves design, plan & budget
CO issued for construction
Reorder quantity set less than 5 out of stocks per month
100% Supply orders pass test on restocking
Fifth HLD:

Construction Project Essentials

Construction Project Essentials

Final Scope & High-

Final Scope & Major Deliverables

				85% of users retrieve supplies in less than 2 minutes
User director approves design, plan & budget	System passed acceptance criteria and user accepts it	Reorder quantity set less than 5 out of stocks per month	100% Supply orders pass test on restocking	Fifth HLD:

Slide 16

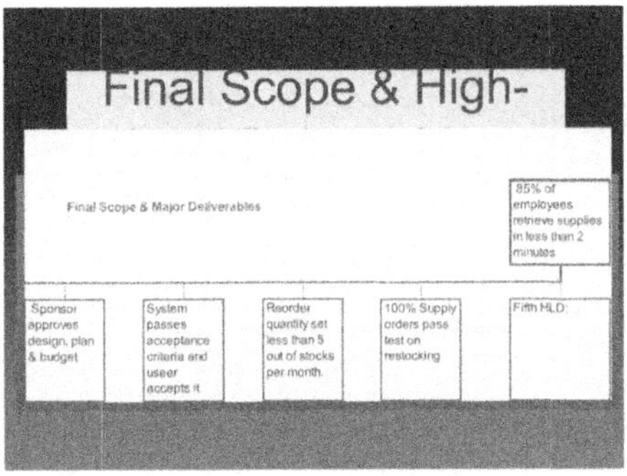
Final Scope & High-
Final Scope & Major Deliverables
85% of employees retrieve supplies in less than 2 minutes
Sponsor approves design, plan & budget
System passes acceptance criteria and useer accepts it
Reorder quantity set less than 5 out of stocks per month.
100% Supply orders pass test on restocking
Fifth HLD:

Construction Project Essentials

Slide 17

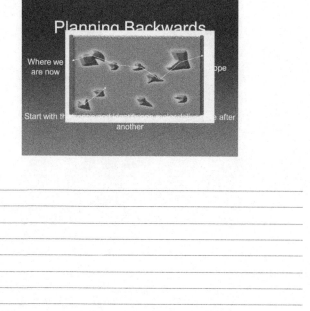

_____
_____
_____
_____
_____
_____
_____
_____
_____
_____
_____
_____
_____
_____
_____
_____

Construction Project Essentials

Slide 19

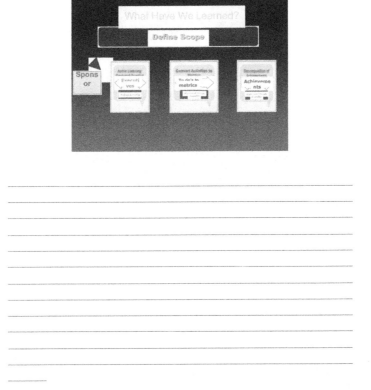

Construction Project Essentials

Slide 21

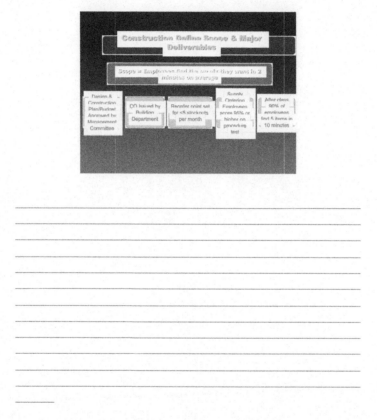

Construction Project Essentials

Slide 22

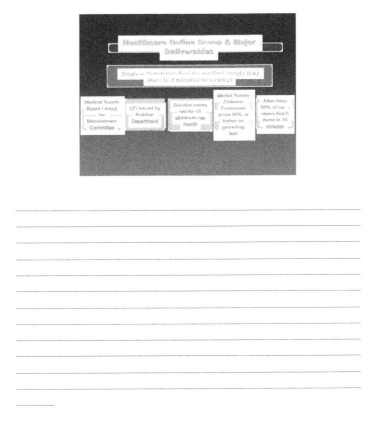

Construction Project Essentials

Slide 23

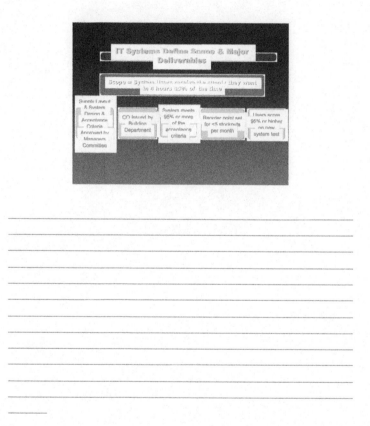

Construction Project Essentials

Slide 24

Construction Project Essentials

Slide 25

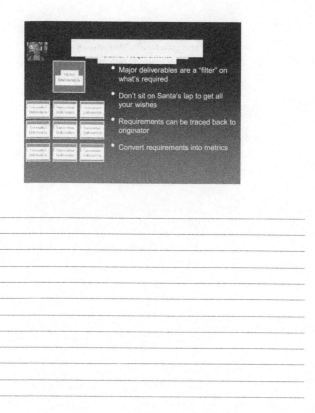

Construction Project Essentials

Slide 26

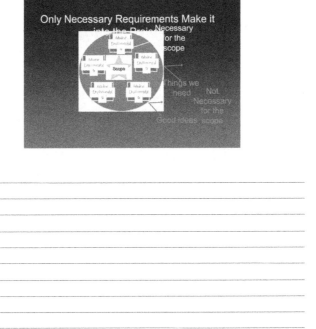

Construction Project Essentials

Slide 27

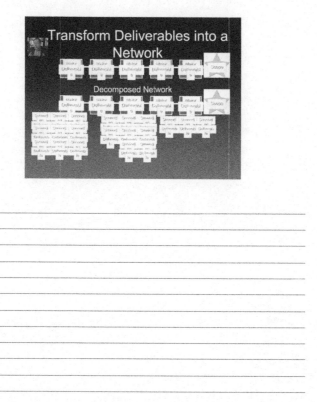

_____
_____
_____
_____
_____
_____
_____
_____
_____
_____
_____
_____
_____
_____

Construction Project Essentials

Construction Project Essentials

Slide 29

Sequential Decomposition

$100,000 in monthly sales

| HLD: Top 5 search positions for 4 keywords in Google | HLD: 100,000 website visitors per month | HLD: 40% visitors return to site within 90 days | HLD: 25,000 orders on website per month |

Components occur in a sequence. Each is a show stopper.
Used for construction, software development, product development

Slide 30

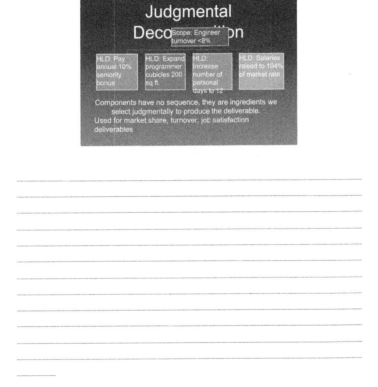

Construction Project Essentials

Slide 31

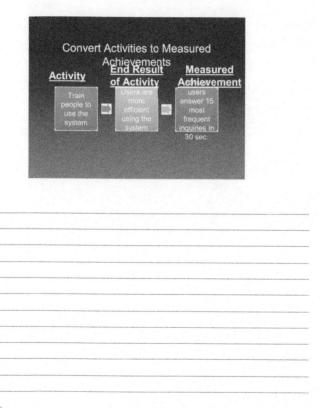

Construction Project Essentials

Convert Activities to Measured Achievements

Activity	End Result of Activity	Measured Achievement
Develop the detailed design of all components with specifications	Management agrees to the design & accepts specs	sign off on design specifications & acceptance criteria

Construction Project Essentials

Slide 33

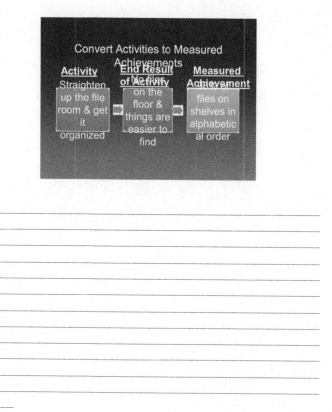

Construction Project Essentials

Slide 34

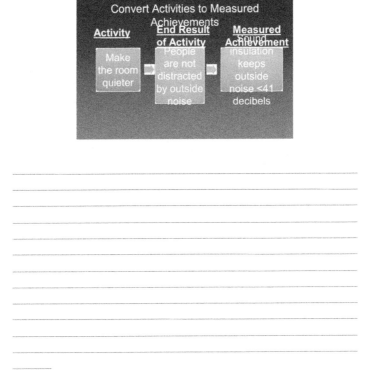

Construction Project Essentials

Slide 35

Construction Project Essentials

Slide 36

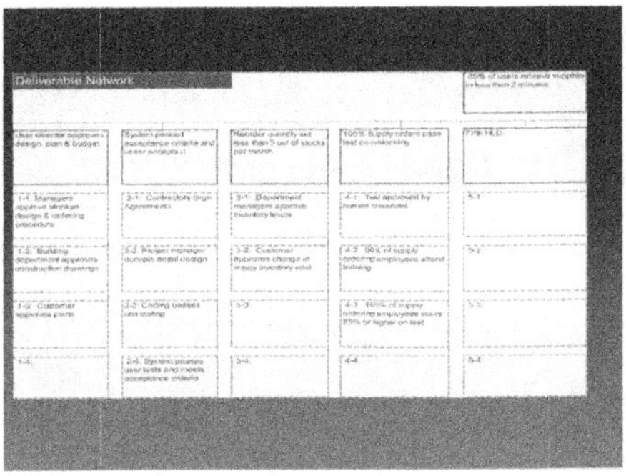

Construction Project Essentials

Slide 37

Construction Project Essentials

Slide 38

Construction Project Essentials

Slide 39

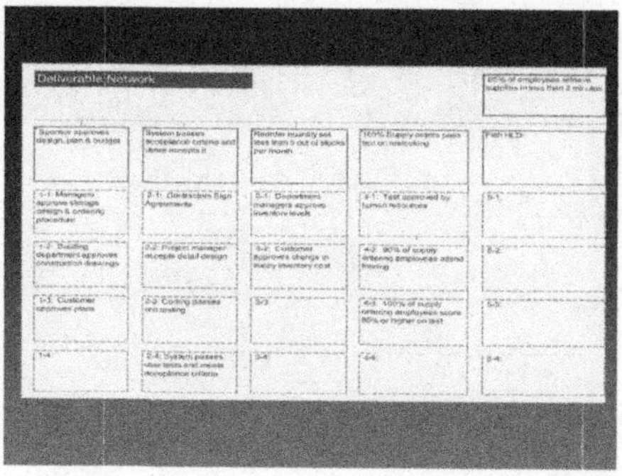

Slide 40Slide 42

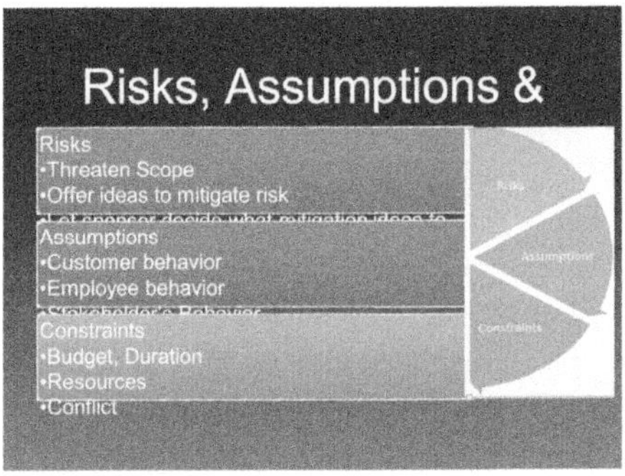

Construction Project Essentials

Slide 43

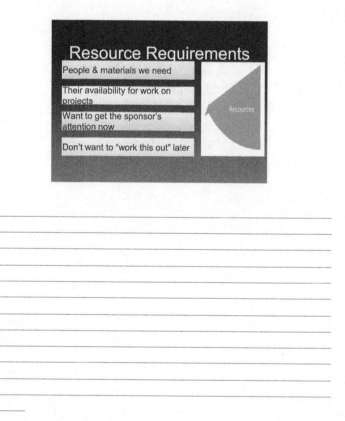

Construction Project Essentials

Slide 44

Construction Project Essentials

Slide 45

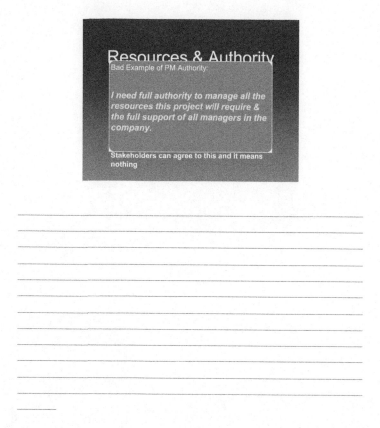

Construction Project Essentials

Slide 46

Construction Project Essentials

Slide 47

Change Control

We want to secure the sponsor's approval on:
- Who can approve what size change
- What documentation is required
- What size change must go to sponsor
- What size change the PM can approve

We want the sponsor to consider not only the change but the impact on all of the following: scope, quality, resources, duration & cost

_____
_____
_____
_____
_____
_____
_____
_____
_____
_____
_____
_____
_____
_____
_____
_____

Construction Project Essentials

Slide 48

Change Control Statement

Good example of change control

The sponsor must approve changes to the scope, any high level deliverable or the overall duration of the project. For every requested change, the PM will estimate the corresponding impact on achievement, cost and duration and document the consequences. The PM will have the authority to sign off on changes that do not affect the Scope, high level deliverables, or overall duration or budget.

Construction Project Essentials

Slide 49

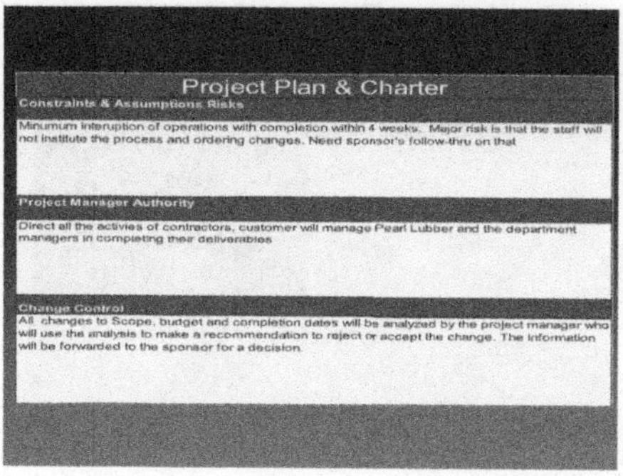

Construction Project Essentials

Slide 50

Resources, Accountability and Authority Structure

Deliverable	Sub-Deliverable Accountability	Work Hours Estimate or contract terms
85% of employees retrieve supplies in less than 2 minutes		
Start		
Sponsor approves design, plan & budget		
1-1: Managers approve storage design & ordering procedure	Pearl Lubber	50
1-2: Building department approves construction drawings	PM	25
1-3: Customer approves plans	PM	5

Construction Project Essentials

Making Project
Presentations
That Persuade &
Influence

- One style presentation is not good for all audiences
- Need to tailor it for the best fit
  - Stakeholder personality style
  - Preferences for how to receive information
  - Need time to consider the information before deciding

Construction Project Essentials

Giving the Presentation

Analyze the audience: Who are they?

- Primary Decision Makers
- Secondary Influencers (staff, subordinates)
- Technical Decision makers
- What are their attitudes about the project?

Delivery of the Presentation:
- Media
- Presentation Techniques
- Delivery Style, Language, Pace

Construction Project Essentials

Personality Types

Live externally Decide on the spot	Live internally Need time to process information
Extraverts	**Introverts**

Construction Project Essentials

Slide 54

Identifying Extraverts & Communicating with Them

- People who think while talking, like to be engaged with people
- Will make decisions on the fly
- Not interested in the detail
- We identify an extravert by observing them:
  - Speak sentence after sentence without any pauses to think
  - Want to hear the end result first before the chronological detail

- Expect them to talk during the presentation; be ready
- Want the information to decide quickly
- Too much detail and you lose them

Construction Project Essentials

Slide 5

Persuading Extraverts

- Be prepared for them to talk and interact
- Will not sit passively and listen
- Plan for an interactive presentation
- You respond to questions
- Best if they reach the "right" answer themselves

_____
_____
_____
_____
_____
_____
_____
_____
_____
_____
_____
_____
_____

Construction Project Essentials

Slide 6

Identifying Introverts & Communicating with Them

- Often pause to think between ideas
- Need time to digest the information
- Want the detail
- If pushed for a decision too quickly it will be no
- We identify an introvert by observing them:
  - Frequent pauses to think before they speak
  - Pause to think before they respond
  - Very interested in detailed information usually chronologically
  - Prefer information in chronological order; Not the big picture

Construction Project Essentials

Slide 7

Persuading Introverts

- Details in advance so they have time to process the info
- Don't push for a decision, wait for it; they need time
- They will listen attentively to the details
- Be prepared for detail-oriented questions
- Be sure your detail is flawless

Construction Project Essentials

Slide 8

Mixed Audiences

- When your audience includes both introverts and extraverts
  - Design your presentations to meet the needs of each of them
  - Introverts get the detail before the meeting
  - Extraverts are given time to talk during the meeting
  - Extraverts want the big picture
  - Project manager is ready to steer the conversation back on track

Construction Project Essentials

Slide 9

Body Language

Extension of our personality

Show confidence

Mannerisms to avoid

video

_____
_____
_____
_____
_____
_____
_____
_____
_____
_____
_____
_____
_____
_____
_____

Construction Project Essentials

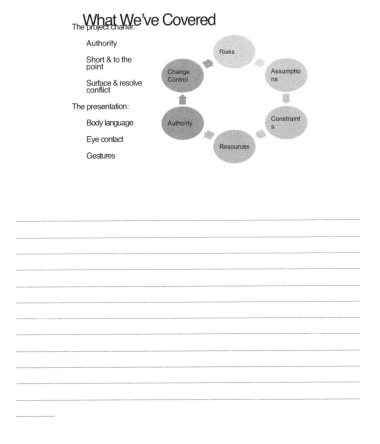

What We've Covered

The project charter:

Authority

Short & to the point

Surface & resolve conflict

The presentation:

Body language

Eye contact

Gestures

Risks

Assumptions

Constraints

Resources

Authority

Change Control

Construction Project Essentials

Slide 11

Communications Plan for Each Stakeholder

Stakeholder	E or I	Comm preference	Design

Construction Project Essentials

Slide 12

Communications Plan for Stakeholder

Stakeholder Analysis and Communications Plan		
Stakeholder Name	Personality Type E or I	Individual Communication Plan

Construction Project Essentials

Slide 13

The Charter Presentation

- First 60 seconds set the tone, but its when you are nervous
- Using visual aids can keep you on track and engage them
- Your body language needs to communicate confidence
- Eye contact makes them pay attention and feel part of it
- Gestures make you more interesting to watch
- Presence the toughest part

_____
_____
_____
_____
_____
_____
_____
_____
_____
_____
_____
_____
_____

Construction Project Essentials

Slide 14

The First 60 Seconds

Composing the introduction

- Grab listeners' attention and avoid too cute
  - Preview main points = tell them what you will say
    Presentation will show how we can reduce cost by 20%
  - Keep it simple but why it is interesting
    Taking a new (proven) approach to improving performance

Identify with audience, understand their hot buttons
Make it personal

Construction Project Essentials

Slide 15

Benefits of Visual Aids

Improve listener understanding
•Announce each main point
•Accentuate & illuminate important ideas

Helps audience follow your "train of thought"
•Provide an outline
•Ensure message is immediately evident

Makes your presentation more memorable
•Helps people see what you mean
•Increases the chances that what you said will be

Key is to make the media a second input not a repeat of what you are saying

Construction Project Essentials

Slide 16

Guidelines for Using Visual Aids

Fonts

Graphics & Design

Color

Nothing smaller than 24 point
High contrast color scheme
Graphs and charts
No decoration
60 seconds per slide

Construction Project Essentials

Slide 17

_____
_____
_____
_____
_____
_____
_____
_____
_____
_____
_____
_____
_____
_____

Construction Project Essentials

Slide 18
Slide 19

Eye Contact

- Powerful Communication Tool
- Connection
- Valuable Feedback
- Timing
- Eye Contact Equality

Construction Project Essentials

Slide 20

Gestures

| Visual Picture |
| Spontaneous |
| Hand Gestures |
| Open Facial Expressions |
| Gestures to Avoid |

Construction Project Essentials

Slide 21

Essentials of Project Management

The backbone of the schedule with success metrics for each task

Hierarchy of deliverables with decomposition down to assignments

The "pieces" we'll use to estimate work and duration

Foundation for tracking, variance analysis

Construction Project Essentials

Work Breakdown Structure

Techniques for creating a strong WBS

The WBS is not a "to do" list	Crafting "right sized" assignments	Using MS Project to build the WBS

Construction Project Essentials

Improve Customer Service
- Reserve training room
- Develop training
- Order snacks for training
- Everyone attends training
- Train employees

These are "to do's"
We want measured
achievements

Construction Project Essentials

95% customer satisfaction by survey	These are clear
R. Smith approves training materials	success metrics
100% employees attend training	that define
90% employees score 80% or higher on end of training exam	expectations

Construction Project Essentials

What Makes a Good WBS?

Team members know what is expected

Each task has an unambiguous measured result

We can estimate the work

The task is within the capabilities of the person

The task is a stretch for the assigned resource

How Big Should Assignments Be?

Assignment Duration:
Usually 2 to 10 days worth of work
Decide how long based on person's ability
Decompose to the "right" size where we can

Expert:
3 weeks

Experienced:
7-10 days

New Team Member:
1-4 days

Construction Project Essentials

Slide 27

Micro-management Does Not = Tight Control

Construction Project Essentials

Slide 28

What You've Learned

How to decompose the WBS	How to define measured achievements
Crafting right size assignments	Using Project software to build the WBS

_____
_____
_____
_____
_____
_____
_____
_____
_____
_____
_____
_____
_____
_____

Construction Project Essentials

Slide 29

Construction Project Essentials

Slide 30

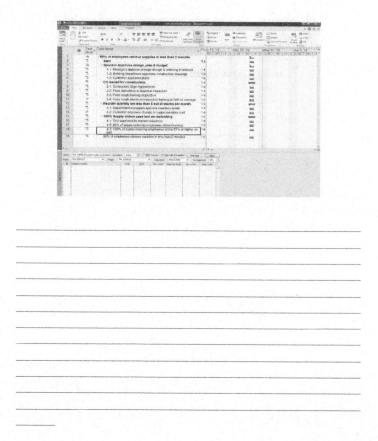

Construction Project Essentials

Slide 31

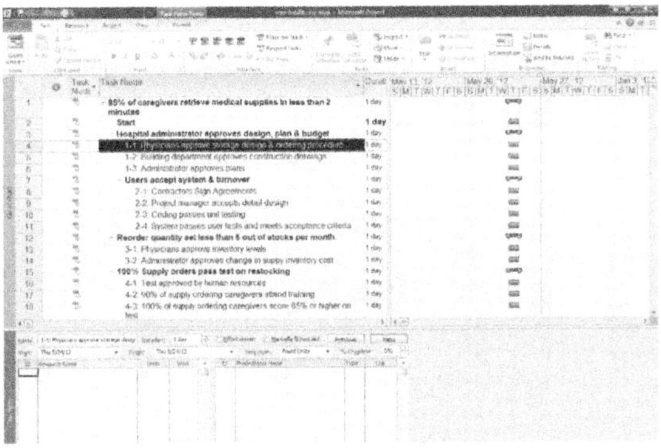

Construction Project Essentials

Slide 32

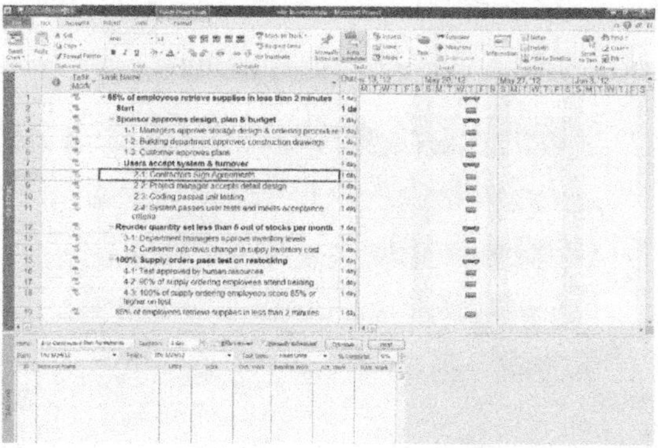

Construction Project Essentials

Let's Build a WBS in the Software

Enter HLDs: Spine of WBS

Subdivide HLDs into sub-achievements

Each is a measured end result

Each conveys a performance expectation

Use approvals when no metric exists

Construction Project Essentials

Slide 34

Essentials of Project Management

Sequencing

Benefits of building a dynamic model	→	Predecessors to control the sequence	→	Spotting danglers in the project plan

| Update schedule in 10 min/week | ← | Model options in minutes | ← | Dynamic scheduling |

Construction Project Essentials

Slide 35

Task Sequencing in a Dynamic Schedule

A

B

C

Tell the software
•The sequence, not the start dates
•Task C can't start until A & B are done

Construction Project Essentials

Rules of Dynamic Scheduling

Dynamic, not static scheduling	Tasks	Network
• No fixed start or finish dates for tasks • We let the software calculate them	A task's start date is controlled by the finish date of its predecessor(s)	• No danglers • 1 endpoint • Every task except summaries have a predecessor

Construction Project Essentials

Predecessor Relationships

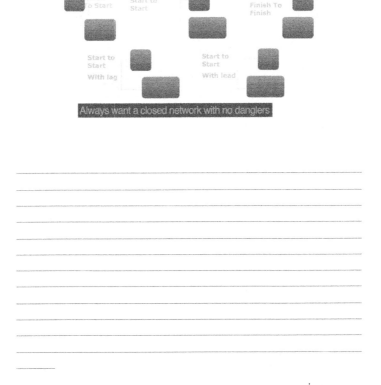

Construction Project Essentials

What You've Learned

- Benefits of building a dynamic
- Predecessors to control the
- Spotting danglers in the project plan

_____
_____
_____
_____
_____
_____
_____
_____
_____
_____
_____
_____
_____
_____

Construction Project Essentials

Slide 39

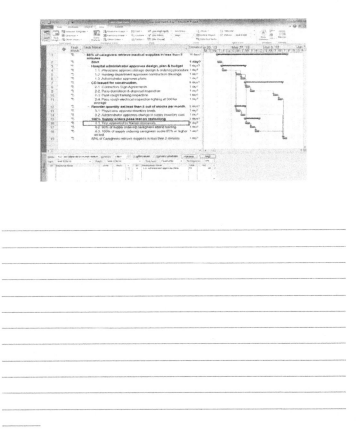

Construction Project Essentials

Slide 40

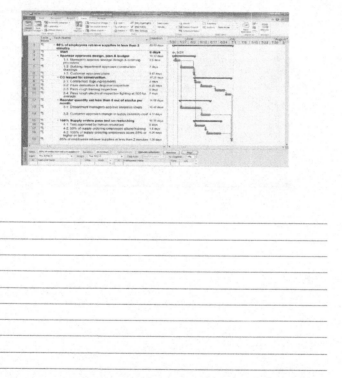

Construction Project Essentials

Slide 41

Construction Project Essentials

Slide 42

———————————————————————————————————
———————————————————————————————————
———————————————————————————————————
———————————————————————————————————
———————————————————————————————————
———————————————————————————————————
———————————————————————————————————
———————————————————————————————————
———————————————————————————————————
———————————————————————————————————
———————————————————————————————————
———————————————————————————————————
———————

Construction Project Essentials

Slide 43

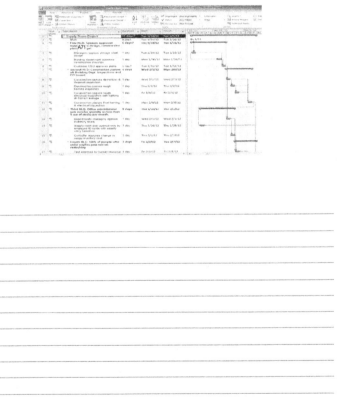

Construction Project Essentials

Slide 44

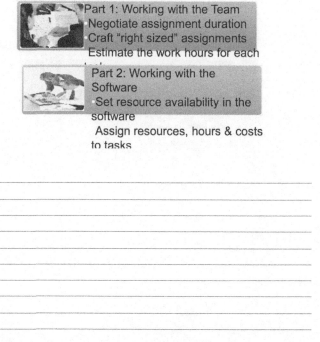

Essentials of Project Management

Part 1: Working with the Team
- Negotiate assignment duration
- Craft "right sized" assignments
- Estimate the work hours for each

Part 2: Working with the Software
- Set resource availability in the software
- Assign resources, hours & costs to tasks

Slide 45

Why We Plan and Track Hours & Costs

We estimate hours and track progress in hours:
- We can spot problems earlier and solve them when they are small
- We can measure progress accurately
- Finish on time

We control contractor and material costs & track them:
- Spot problems early and fix them
- Control expenditures accurately
- Calculate the cost of all change orders
- Finish within budget

_____
_____
_____
_____
_____
_____
_____
_____
_____
_____
_____
_____
_____
_____
_____

Construction Project Essentials

Slide 46

Resources, Work & Duration

For every achievement in the project plan we'll have:
- Resource availability (units) and the cost of each person
- Work estimates

We set up the "resource sheet," entering the person's name, hourly cost and their availability in FTE units (1.0 or 100% is a full time person, 0.5 or 50% is half time, etc.)

Then we assign the person to a task or tasks, enter the work estimate and their availability and the software will calculate the duration

Construction Project Essentials

Slide 47

Materials and Contractor Costs

For every achievement in the project plan we'll have:
- Cost of major materials needed to complete the task (PCs, cable, etc.) kinds of costs to the resource sheet or consultant contractors hired to complete the task
  - Fixed costs like a contract for $2,000 for professional services
  - Material costs like 10 PC's that each cost $850
  - Per use costs: air travel or equipment rental which

We assign the costs to a task and enter the fixed cost or the number of units we plan to use. The software will then calculate the project cost each week.

Construction Project Essentials

Slide 48

Estimating Process

1. Discuss risk, then estimate hours with the team member assigned to each task

    1. Pessimistic, Best Guess, Optimistic

2. Use the work package form for estimating work and cost

3. Estimate cost with contractors and outside vendors

    1. Try for a fixed price contract which reduces project risk

        1. Enter that cost in the fixed cost column.

        2. If time and materials, set up the contractor as an employee with rate

    2. Use a work package to detail the requirements

    — Make the agreement into a contract (you may need legal help)

Construction Project Essentials

Slide 49

Team Member Work Package: Estimating, Risk & Process Controls	
WBS Number:	
Measured Deliverable	100% of supply room users pass test on supply procedure
Responsibility of:	Trainer
Accountable to:	PM
Date Approved:	23-May
Availability for the assignment	Full time for three weeks
Approach Statement:	Develop a test of the new inventory procedure and secure the approval of Pearl Lubber and the department managers of the curriculum and test
Input Deliverable(s):	New work flow for the supply room
Output Deliverable(s):	Test results sent to managers

Who is accountable to whom for what

Construction Project Essentials

Slide 51

Risk issues:	Pessimistic Factors		Optimistic Factors	
	Employees will not attend training so additional classes		Managers pressure people to attend first class	
Assumptions:	Test will measure understanding of the new process			
Documentation & developmental checkpoints	Approval by human resources			
Work (hours/days):	Pessimistic	Best Guess		Optimistic
	50 Hrs	45		35
Estimated Duration:				44.1

Risk & Estimating

Construction Project Essentials

Slide 52

Material Quantity & Cost:	None
Change Control Record	
Actual hours/duration	

Keeping track of changes as well as actual hours makes
the work package a great tool for estimating
similar tasks on the next project

_____

_____

_____

_____

_____

_____

_____

_____

_____

_____

_____

_____

_____

Construction Project Essentials

Slide 53

Construction Project Essentials

Slide 54

Expectations & Padding Estimates

Why do team members pad their estimates?

To protect themselves from blame

This blame avoidance is most severe when they think:
* "The scope will change twice a week"
* "The assignment has unforeseen challenges"
* "The boss will give me a #1 priority task"
* "They will cut my estimate in half"

Construction Project Essentials

Slide 4

Construction Project Essentials

Slide 5

Construction Project Essentials

Slide 6

Construction Project Essentials

Slide 7

Construction Project Essentials

Slide 8

Construction Project Essentials

Slide 9

Essentials of Project Management

Use critical path to shorten duration and spot tasks that have slack (float)

Use the software to model options for doing the project faster and cheaper

Present a plan & tradeoffs for faster & cheaper

_____
_____
_____
_____
_____
_____
_____
_____
_____
_____
_____
_____
_____
_____

Construction Project Essentials

Slide 10

Critical Path Technique

Analyze the critical path:
- Critical path=longest path. Controls project duration
- Use it to shorten duration:
  - If we shorten duration of a critical path task we shorten project duration

_____

_____

_____

_____

_____

_____

_____

_____

_____

_____

_____

_____

_____

_____

_____

Construction Project Essentials

Slide 11

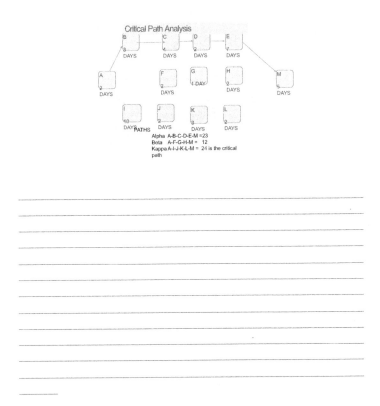

Construction Project Essentials

Slide 12

Principal Tradeoffs: Gives Executives Choices

Model 6 options:
- 3 to finish earlier
- 10% earlier
- 20% earlier
- 30% earlier
- 3 to cost less
- 10% cheaper
- 20% cheaper
- 30% cheaper

Tradeoffs always have two sides and a BUT

Construction Project Essentials

Slide 13

Prepare Your Tradeoffs before the Meeting

Quantify tradeoffs like:
- Earlier finish date but more resources
- Earlier finish date but lower scope

Lower budget but cheaper resources

Lower budget but lower scope

Construction Project Essentials

Slide 14

Modeling Tradeoffs

Options for reducing the duration or the budget
•We shorten the duration by:
  • Adding resources to critical path tasks
  • Reducing the achievement
•We reduce the budget by:
  • Using less expensive resources
  • Reducing the achievement
•We reduce time & cost by reducing scope & deliverables

Construction Project Essentials

Slide 15

Duration Tradeoffs

Adding a resource, we finish task B in half the time and it does not cost more

Construction Project Essentials

Tradeoffs that scale back deliverables

Task Name	Total Cost	Apr 3, '11	Apr 10, '11	Apr 17, '11	Apr 24, '11	
		S M T W T F S	S M T W T F S	S M T W T F S	S M T W T F S	
<5% of customers call back about the same issue	$4,400.00					Ma

Reduce scope & deliverables to decrease budget & duration

Task Name	Total Cost	Apr 3, '11	Apr 10, '11	Apr
		S M T W T F S	S M T W T F S	S M
<10% of customers call back about the same issue	$2,900.00			Mon

_____
_____
_____
_____
_____
_____
_____
_____
_____
_____
_____
_____
_____
_____
_____

Construction Project Essentials

What You've Learned

•Optimize, then model tradeoffs	•Use critical path to shorten duration duration	•Present tradeoff options to the boss	•Present a plan & get it approved

Demo

Construction Project Essentials

Slide 18

Construction Project Essentials

Slide 19

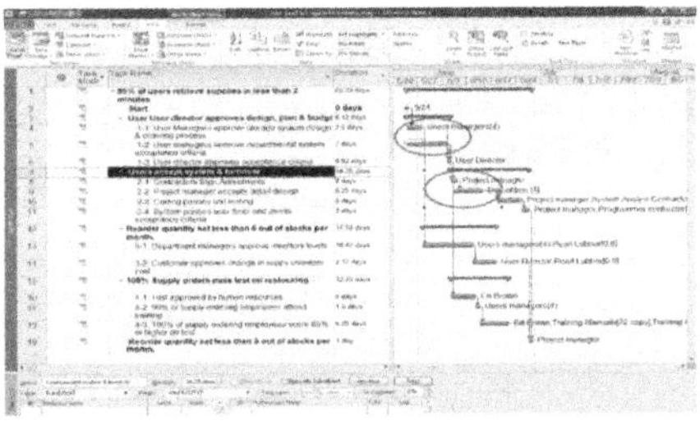

Construction Project Essentials

Slide 20

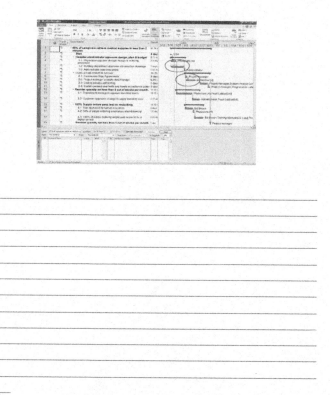

Construction Project Essentials

Slide 21

Construction Project Essentials

Slide 22

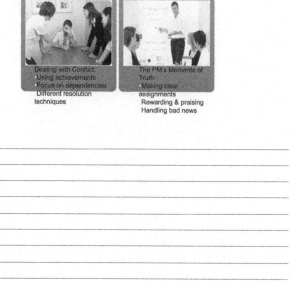

Essentials of Project Management

Dealing with Conflict:
•Using achievements
•Focus on dependencies
Different resolution
techniques

The PM's Moments of
Truth:
•Making clear
assignments
Rewarding & praising
Handling bad news

Construction Project Essentials

1st Moment of Truth:
Making Clear Assignments

No Guessing

Problem
Solving Skills

Less Blame
Avoidance

Personally
Accountable

Team
Member
Trust

_____
_____
_____
_____
_____
_____
_____
_____
_____
_____
_____
_____
_____
_____

Construction Project Essentials

Slide 24

2nd Moment of Truth:
Feedback

The PM's praise has value when:
- Public
- Consistent & justified
- Measurable & defined beforehand
- Specific about outstanding

The PM's praise loses value if:
- Given to everyone
- No tie to demonstrated performance
- Given to avoid hurt feelings

_____
_____
_____
_____
_____
_____
_____
_____
_____
_____
_____
_____
_____
_____
_____

Construction Project Essentials

3rd Moment of Truth:
Dealing with Bad News

Bad News From the Sponsor
- Will PM let blame fall on the team?
- Or insulate the team from blame?
- Does team need to avoid blame?

Bad News From a Team Member
- PM gets angry & punishes the person
- This insures they delay revealing problems

Construction Project Essentials

Slide 26

PM Style & Conflict

- Anticipate Conflict
- ID Sources of Conflict in the Charter
- When Conflict Flares: Separate Personality from Issues
- Preserve the Achievement Contract

Construction Project Essentials

Techniques

Different Techniques for Dealing with Different Situations

- Compromising - Everybody wins a little in negotiated solution
- Confronting - Take the time to analyze the issue
- Forcing - PM decides and makes it stick
- Smoothing - Avoid the problem, gloss over it
- Withdrawal - PM spends no time on

Construction Project Essentials

Slide 29

Compromising

Use when:
- Both parties need to win
- Can take time to craft mutually agreeable solution
  Issue is important enough to justify PM's time

Construction Project Essentials

Confronting the Issue and Working it Out

Use when:
- Both parties can't win
- There is time available
- You want to reduce cost of project
- You have confidence in both parties

Construction Project Essentials

Slide 31

Forcing a Solution

Use when:
- One party is right
- Relationships are unimportant
- A fast decision needs to be made

Construction Project Essentials

Slide 32

Smoothing

Use when:
- Trying to keep the peace
- Both solutions are adequate
- Trying to save time
- Small impact on project

Construction Project Essentials

Slide 33

Withdrawal

Use when:
- One party can't win
- Low stakes
- High stakes but PM unprepared

Construction Project Essentials

Slide 34

Focus on Deliverable not Personalities

- They don't have to be friends to finish the deliverable
- Aim to diminish the impact on the project and its deliverables
- Be certain they are seeing beyond personalities to the project and performance issues
- Enforce professional conduct
- Stifle personal attacks

Construction Project Essentials

Slide 35

What You've Learned

Dealing with Conflict	PM's Moments of Truth
•Using achievements •Focus on dependencies •Conflict resolution	•Make clear assignments •Handle bad news •Reward & criticism

Construction Project Essentials

Slide 36

Conflict & MOT on our small project

_____
_____
_____
_____
_____
_____
_____
_____
_____
_____
_____
_____
_____
_____
_____

Construction Project Essentials

Slide 37

Essentials of Project Management

Tracking Team Member Progress	The Estimate to Complete Data Needed for Accurate Status Reports
Use the Software to Track Progress Before the Status Meeting, not During	Model Variance & Solutions for the Sponsor

_____
_____
_____
_____
_____
_____
_____
_____
_____
_____
_____
_____
_____

Construction Project Essentials

Slide 38

Baseline & Forecasted Variances Data

Baseline (Originally Approved Schedule/Budget) to Actual

Basis of comparison

We gather status data from the team members who report hours worked by task and an estimate of hours to complete the task

We enter that data into software and assess variances vs. baseline and assess the impact of the actuals on budget and duration of the project

Construction Project Essentials

Slide 39

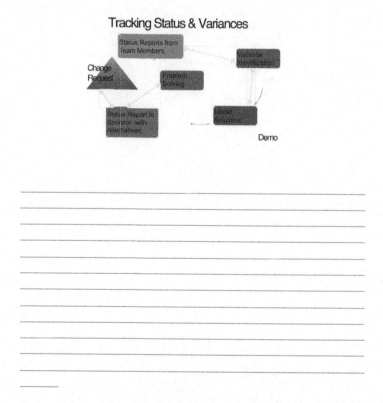

Tracking Status & Variances

Demo

Construction Project Essentials

Slide 40

Change Request

Follow the change control
policy in the charter

PM analyzes impact of
change in the software on

- Scope
- Duration
- Cost
- Risk
- Quality

Construction Project Essentials

Slide 41

Construction Project Essentials

Slide 42

Construction Project Essentials

Construction Project Essentials

Slide 44

Construction Project Essentials

Slide 45

Change Request from the Template

Project name: supply Room	Brief description of change being requested: Add a work area in the supply room with desk, ethernet connection and printer
Submitted by:	
Date: 6/23	Approval level: Project sponsor
Impact on Scope	No impact, not necessary to achieve the scope
Impact on Cost	$2000 increase
Impact on Schedule	Adds 3 days to the completion date
Impact on Quality	No impact.
Project manager's evaluation and recommendation on _6_/_24_/___ Sponsor decision on __/__/__	Reject

Construction Project Essentials

Slide 46

Construction Project Essentials

Slide 47

_____
_____
_____
_____
_____
_____
_____
_____
_____
_____
_____
_____
_____
_____
_____

Construction Project Essentials

Slide 48

_____
_____
_____
_____
_____
_____
_____
_____
_____
_____
_____
_____
_____
_____
_____
_____

Construction Project Essentials

Slide 49

Construction Project Essentials

Slide 50

Status Report from Template

Status Report Worksheet		Without Corrective Action			Applying Corrective Action
Task Number	Name	Current variance	Forecasted variance	Impact on project cost & duration	Corrective Action Options & Impact
4	1-1: User Managers approve storage	6 days	8 days	4,000	Project sponsor need to force a decision by the managers on the new design

_____
_____
_____
_____
_____
_____
_____
_____
_____
_____
_____
_____
_____
_____
_____
_____
_____

About the Author

Dick Billows, PMP, GCA is President of The Hampton Group, Inc., (4PM.com) specializing in project and program management. He has more than twenty years of project management experience managing hundreds of successful projects as both a management and systems consulting partner with an international accounting firm and internally within a Fortune 100 organization.

His professional career began with two years as a financial analyst on Wall Street followed by six years as a consulting engineer, analyst then project manager, leading implementation projects throughout the US and abroad. Dick served as the Director of Management Systems for a major insurance company, leading a corporate reengineering effort. Then he served as Regional General Manager for the 14 state Rocky Mountain region of a Fortune 100 drug company, managing a portfolio of marketing, system and operational improvement projects that led to a tripling of revenues and profits in two years. He launched numerous new products and several subsidiary business ventures. Next, Dick was the partner-in-charge of Rocky Mountain management consulting for a big ten accounting firm, managing hundreds of installation and system development projects for clients. Dick's project management experience ranges from PC systems for small start-up organizations to network solutions for multi-national companies. More recent deliverables have come with e-commerce and web-based learning systems development.

In 1986, Dick formed the Hampton Group, Inc. and has assisted numerous organizations in their project management including: Siemens, NASA, Intel, Citicorp, Disney, GXS, ConocoPhillips, Health South, Kaiser Permanente, EDS,

Construction Project Essentials

Hewlett-Packard, Kodak, Marathon Oil, Federal Reserve Bank, Broadcom ,Oracle, Bethlehem Steel, Bell South, First Data Corporation and US Dept. of Energy as well as smaller organizations like Candy's Tortilla Factory and Colorado Mountain Development.

Dick was a member of the advisory board that developed the Gartner IT Project Management Certification. Dick has a BA in Economics and Statistics from Johns Hopkins University, an MBA from the University of Colorado and did three years of doctoral work in Organizational Behavior, also at the University of Colorado.

Dick is also the author of: Essentials of Project Management, 11th edition 2013; Project Manager's Knowledge Base, 11th edition 2013; Advanced IT Project Techniques, 6th edition, 2013; Advanced Construction Project Techniques, 5th edition, 2013, Program and Portfolio Management, 9th edition, 2011 and Advanced Healthcare Project Techniques, 3rd edition, 2013.

He is a frequent speaker at Project Management Institute Symposiums and writes the monthly PMTalk newsletter and the 4PM blog.

Made in United States
Orlando, FL
26 July 2022